CREATIVE SONGWRI[TING]
16 Practical Tips for Sp[icing Up] Chords & Taking You[r...]

BY TROY NELSON

HOW TO GET THE AUDIO	3
INTRODUCTION	5
SECTION 1: THE CREATIVE SPARK	**6**
CHAPTER 1: THE POWER OF A SINGLE CHORD	6
CHAPTER 2: THE CLIFFS ON RIFFS	10
CHAPTER 3: MELODY IS KING!	15
CHAPTER 4: LET VIBE BE YOUR GUIDE	19
SECTION 2: SPICING UP BLAND CHORDS	**23**
CHAPTER 5: USING "UNEXPECTED" CHORDS	23
CHAPTER 6: CHORD EMBELLISHMENT	29
CHAPTER 7: OPEN-STRING DRONES	33
CHAPTER 8: OCTAVES AND DOUBLE STOPS	37
CHAPTER 9: ARPEGGIOS	43
CHAPTER 10: 10TH INTERVALS	46
CHAPTER 11: HARMONIC RHYTHM	50
SECTION 3: WRITING PARTS TO FIT THE SONG	**54**
CHAPTER 12: GENRE-SPECIFIC GUITAR PARTS	54
CHAPTER 13: PICKING A KEY	60
CHAPTER 14: MAJOR OR MINOR?	66
CHAPTER 15: BUILDING GUITAR PARTS AROUND A BASS LINE	70
CHAPTER 16: BUILDING GUITAR PARTS AROUND A DRUM GROOVE	74
MOVING FORWARD	78

ISBN: 9798708188199   Copyright © 2021 Troy Nelson Music LLC
International Copyright Secured. All Rights Reserved.

No part of this publication may be reproduced without the written consent of the publisher, Troy Nelson Music LLC. Unauthorized copying, arranging, adapting, recording, Internet posting, public performance, or other distribution of the printed or recorded music in this publication is an infringement of copyright. Infringers are liable under the law.

HOW TO GET THE AUDIO

The audio files for this book are available for free as downloads or streaming on *troynelsonmusic.com*.

We are available to help you with your audio downloads and any other questions you may have. Simply email *help@troynelsonmusic.com*.

See below for the recommended ways to listen to the audio:

Download Audio Files (Zipped)	Stream Audio Files
• Download Audio Files (Zipped)	• Recommended for CELL PHONES & TABLETS
• Recommended for COMPUTERS on WiFi	• Bookmark this page
• A ZIP file will automatically download to the default "downloads" folder on your computer	• Simply tap the PLAY button on the track you want to listen to
• Recommended: download to a desktop/laptop computer *first*, then transfer to a tablet or cell phone	• Files also available for streaming or download at *soundcloud.com/troynelsonbooks*
• Phones & tablets may need an "unzipping" app such as iZip, Unrar or Winzip	
• Download on WiFi for faster download speeds	

To download the companion audio files for this book, visit: troynelsonmusic.com/audio-downloads/

INTRODUCTION

If you've been writing songs for a while, then you've probably heard someone say, "The only rule in songwriting is there are no rules." While that's certainly true—songwriting is a form of self-expression, after all—we still need some sort of framework and a set of guidelines to help us achieve the best results, especially if the goal is to appeal to a mass audience.

Creative Songwriting on Guitar was written to teach you, the songwriter, how to use the instrument to spark fresh ideas, spice up chords and progressions you already know, and compose guitar parts that fit the musical styles and ensembles that you're working in. What you won't find in this book is a section on song structure, lyric writing, or music theory; instead, *Creative Songwriting on Guitar* is about helping you find inspiration in new ideas and enhancing the songwriting tools that you already have at your disposal. While many methods teach songwriting from a theoretical perspective, this book takes a practical, hands-on approach, which includes over 125 playable musical examples and audio demonstrations.

Creative Songwriting on Guitar is divided into three main sections. Section 1 is devoted to helping you find the elusive "creative spark." If you're currently experiencing writer's block, then you won't want to skip this section, which devotes four chapters to song-starters—everything from chords and riffs to melody and "vibe."

Section 2 is where you'll find new ways to approach old ideas. Tired of using the same three or four chords in your progressions? Here, you'll discover new chords to keep your listeners' attention, ways to embellish chords you already know, and how to incorporate open strings to create interesting harmonies. We'll also go in-depth on other songwriting tools like double stops, arpeggios, and 10th intervals, all of which can be used to add "ear candy" to your compositions.

Lastly, Section 3 is dedicated to helping you create the right guitar part for the moment. After all, songwriting isn't always a personal endeavor; someday, you might find yourself composing music for film or television, where it's important to know how to write for multiple genres and to create various moods with your music, or playing in a band where the drummer and bass player are also contributing songwriters. This section's five chapters will help you succeed in any scenario you might find yourself in as a songwriter or composer, whether it's picking the right key for a song, composing a guitar part for a specific genre, or locking in with a bass or drum groove.

SECTION 1: THE CREATIVE SPARK

One thing that all songwriters encounter, whether they admit it or not, is writer's block. After all, even the most proficient creator types have days—even weeks or months—when they struggle to come up with a good song idea ("good" in their minds, at least).

If you've experienced writer's block firsthand, I hope you take comfort in knowing that you're not alone—we all go through phases of low productivity. Fortunately for us, the guitar offers a deep well of creative ideas; we just have to know where to tap into it. In this section, I offer up four ideas to help spark your creativity.

CHAPTER 1: THE POWER OF A SINGLE CHORD

As guitarists, we all have our favorite chords. Some chords have a certain sound, or vibe, that just hits us a certain way and can really set the mood, while others have a certain power and energy that work well with a specific guitar or amp setting. As a songwriter and composer, one thing I like to do is exploit the best parts of my favorite chords and turn them into songs. In other words, I examine why I like a specific chord—whether it's the heft of the low end or the ringing of one or more open strings—and create entire riffs or chord progressions around that sonic attribute.

OPEN-STRING HARMONIES
For example, one of my all-time favorite chords is an open Fmaj7sus2 chord:

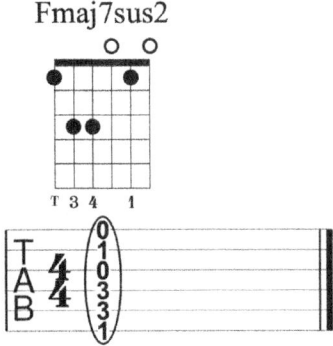

This is essentially and F chord with a couple of open strings. Although it's difficult to voice, I love the sound of the open G and high-E strings against the sonic heft of the fretted pitches, particularly the low tonic note (F) on string 6. So, what I'll do is find other chords that contain these same qualities and create chord progressions based around that one chord, Fmaj7sus2.

In the example on the next page, an Fmaj7sus2–C–Am7–G progression (IV–I–vi–V in C major) is created around the qualities of the Fmaj7sus2 chord. Notice that three of the four chords—Fmaj7sus2, C, and Am7—contain the open G and high-E strings, which maintain the sonic vibe of the chord that launched the progression, Fmaj7sus2. Additionally, the C note on fret 1 of string 2 is maintained throughout nearly the entire progression; in fact, the only time it disappears is when the Gsus4 chord moves to the G triad to signal a return to the top of the progression.

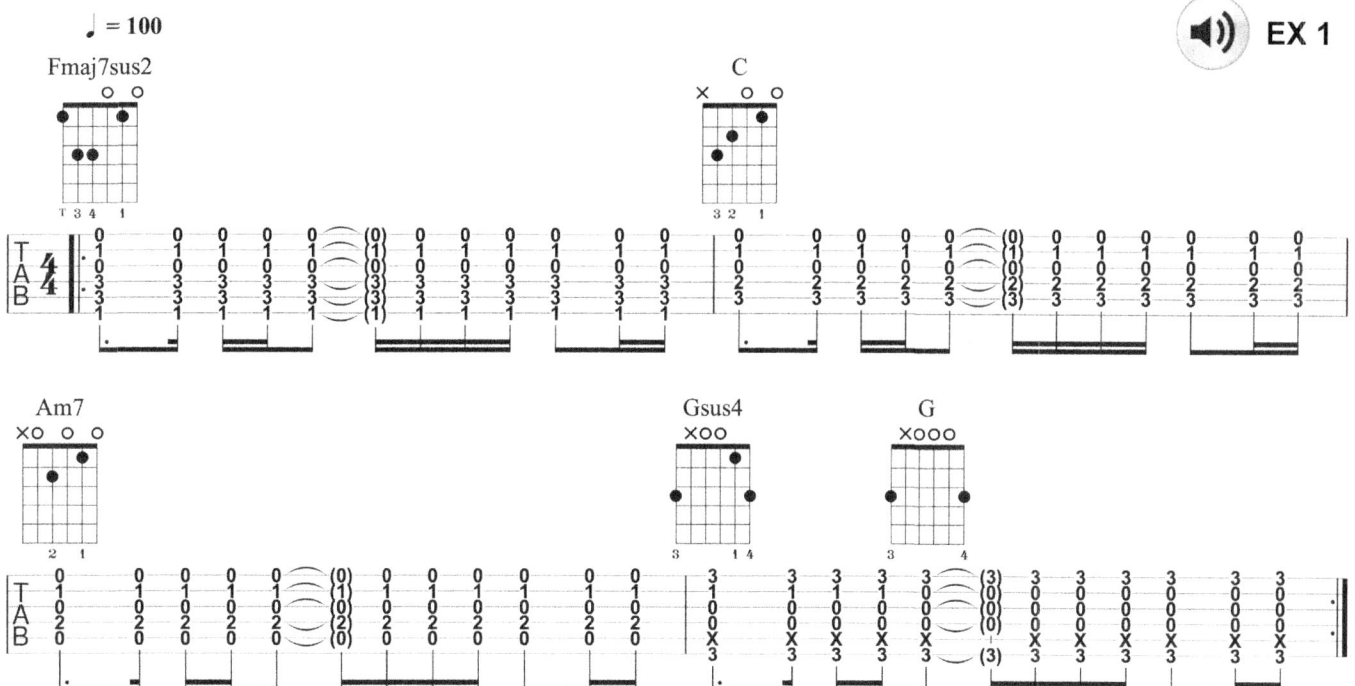

Our next example also prominently features the open G and high-E strings. However, notice in bar 2 that, unlike the previous example, this progression, Dsus2–Am7–Fmaj7sus2–G6(no3rd) (iv–i–VI–VII in A minor), strays from open position by shifting the Fmaj7sus2 voicing up two frets for the G6(no3rd) chord change, which also includes the open G and high-E strings.

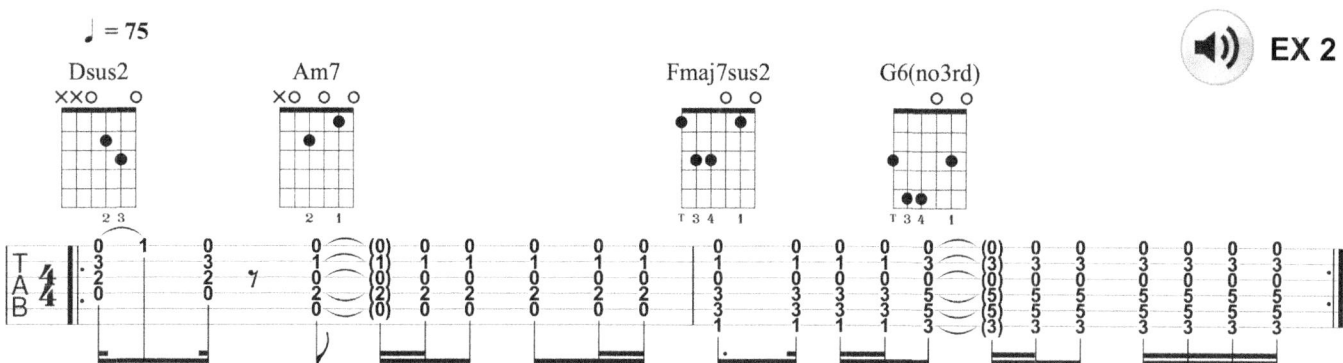

BASS-NOTE SHIFTING

Chord progressions are not the only thing that we can create from the qualities of a single chord. On the contrary, some great single-note arpeggiations and riffs are just waiting to be discovered. All it takes is a little experimentation.

In our next example, the upper-portion of the Fmaj7sus2 chord is used as a springboard to an arpeggio-based riff. Notice all that is happening here is some bass-note shifting (the upper portion of the chord remains unchanged), which creates some great-sounding harmonies (the chord frames above the staff represent the changes implied by the riff).

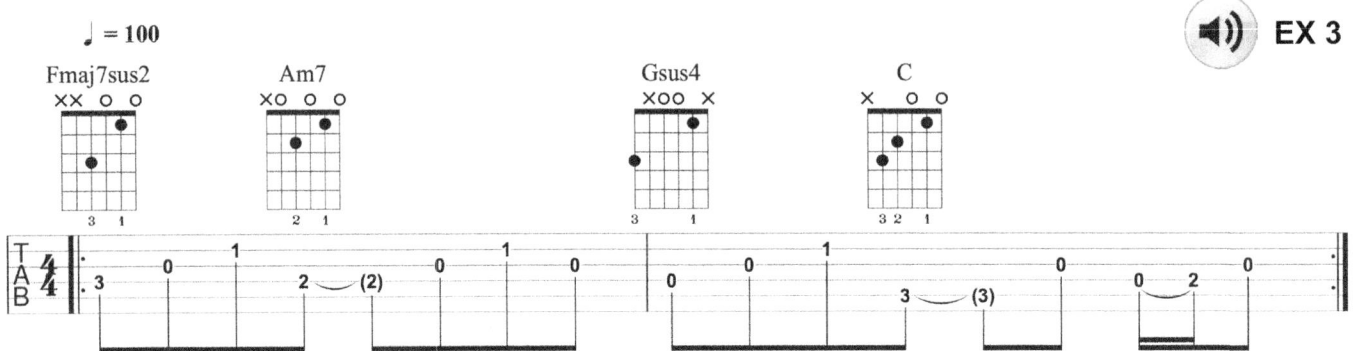

Now let's try another chord. If you've been playing guitar long, then you're aware of how many different ways you can voice an open G chord. I use several myself, depending on the music context, but my favorite is the one below.

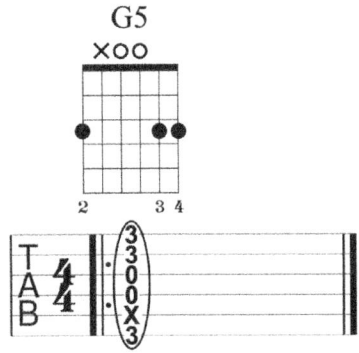

Technically, this chord isn't a standard G triad; it's actually an open G5 power chord. If you're unfamiliar, a *power chord* is a two-note chord comprised of just the root and 5th of the scale—in this case, G major. Meanwhile, a common triad, like G, contains *three* notes of the scale—the root, 3rd, and 5th.

I like this chord for two reasons: 1) it's powerful, and 2) it's stable. Many voicings of open G major include the low B note (the 3rd) on fret 2 of string 5. The problem I have with these voicings is the slight dissonance, or "rub," caused by this note and the low G (fret 3, string 6) ringing together. Since the G5 voicing omits this note (B), the problem is solved!

With that bit of music theory out of the way, let's take a look at a few ways we can use the qualities of the G5 chord to compose some stellar progressions and riffs. In our first example, notice that, as the bass notes of the chords move stepwise down the G major scale—G–F#–E–D–C–B—the notes on top never change; in other words, they continue to maintain the upper portion of the original G5 chord.

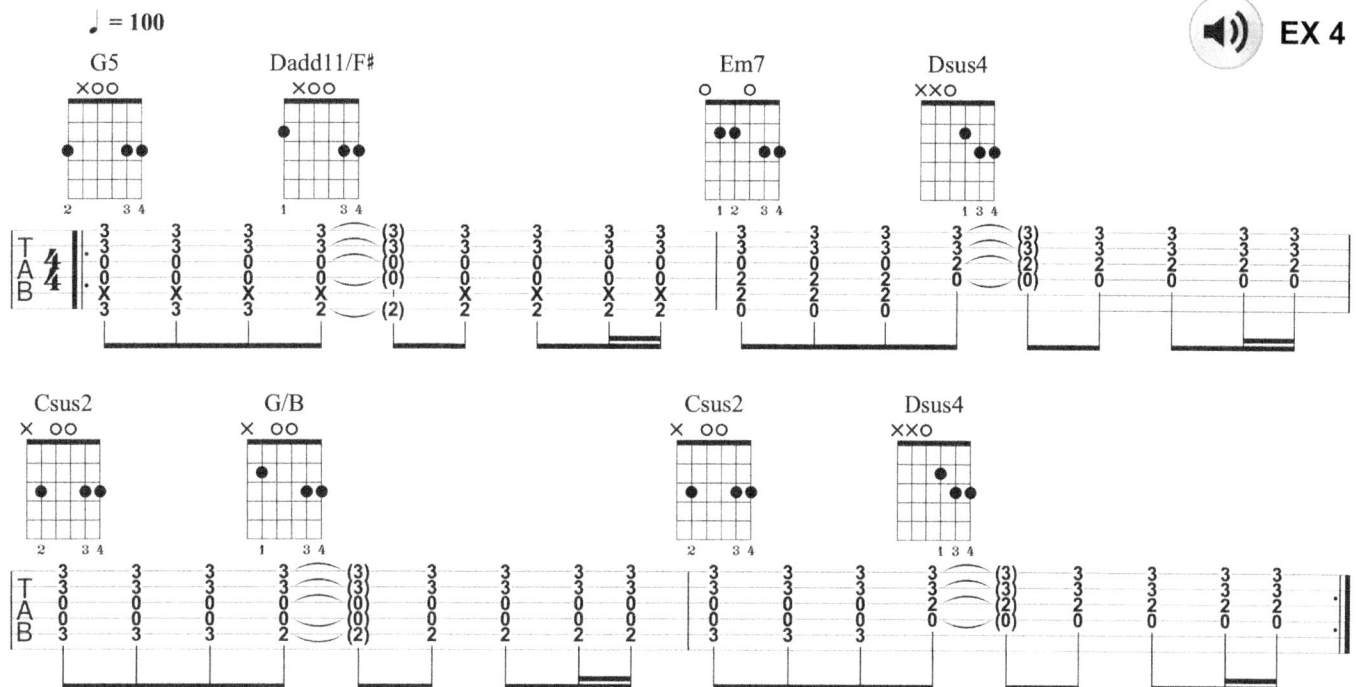

We can use this type of bass movement to create some great riffs, as well. Like our previous example, the open G5 chord is the catalyst for the riff below. Notice that, as the bass notes shift (G–C–E–D–C), a repetitive six-note melody (G–D–G–F#–D–G) is played in a syncopated rhythm on top. At first glance, this four-chord riff might look complex, but closer inspection reveals an idea based around one simple chord: G5.

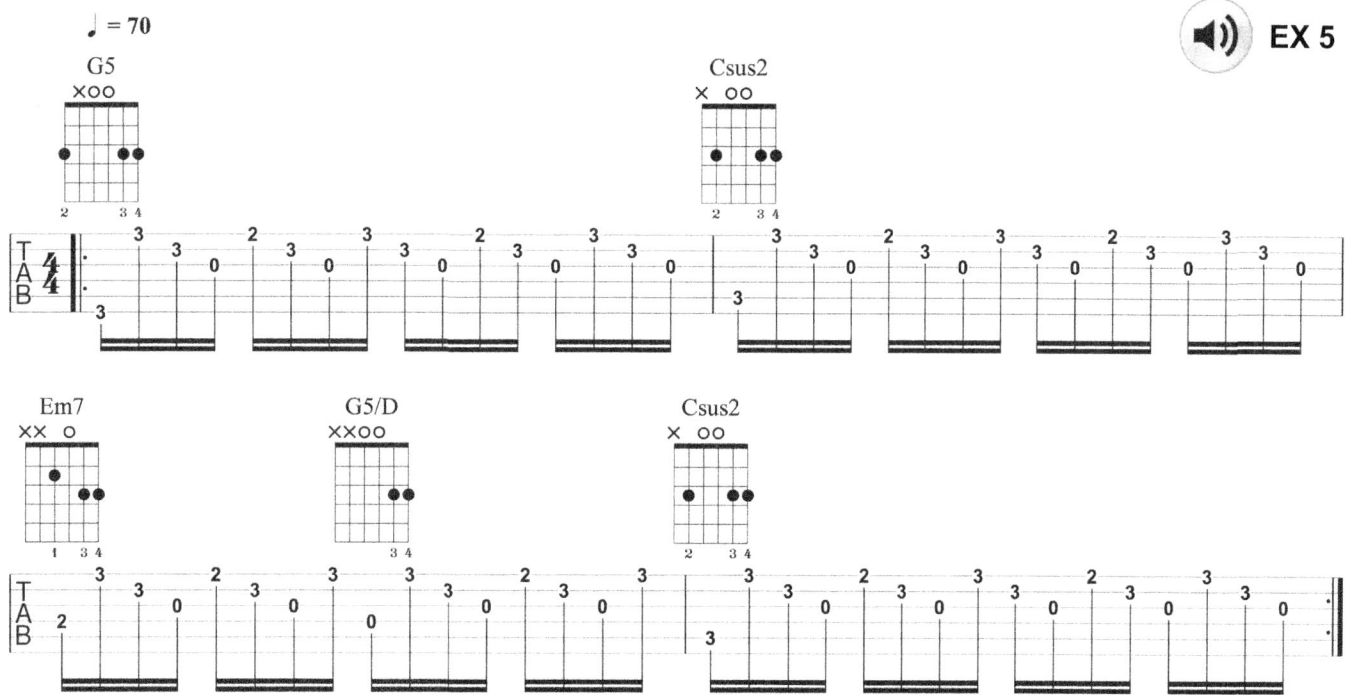

Once you have your idea, the next step is to determine where to use it in your song, whether it's as an introduction, verse, chorus, or some other section. Heck, if the idea is strong enough, it could be the foundation of your entire composition.

CHAPTER 2: THE CLIFFS ON RIFFS

We briefly discussed guitar riffs in the previous chapter, and now we're going to dive a little deeper into the subject and learn how small ideas can be transformed into full-blown songs. If you're unfamiliar, a *guitar riff* is a broad term that encompasses anything that outlines a song's harmony without being a straight (i.e., strummed) performance of the chord progression.

Most riffs are comprised of arpeggios, single-note lines, or double stops—or a combination of these elements and others—and typically come in lengths of two or four bars that are repeated several times to create an instrumental "hook." In this section, we'll talk about how you can create your own riffs and apply them to your songs.

SINGLE-NOTE RIFFS

Some of the most beloved guitar riffs of all time are of the single-note variety, including "Sweet Child O' Mine" (Guns N' Roses), "Day Tripper" (The Beatles), "Beat It" (Michael Jackson), and "Crazy Train" (Ozzy Osbourne), among many others. If you've never written your own guitar riff, don't worry—the process is easier than you think. Let's get started…

As mentioned in the introduction, a guitar riff can be constructed from many different elements, but let's start with single notes. And, to make the process even easier, let's start with something we've already covered: the G chord.

Below is a two-bar riff in the key of G major that uses an open G chord as "home base." Although we're not strumming the full chord, we're still using notes from it, particularly the root, G (fret 3, string 6), as well as other notes from the G major scale (G–A–B–C–D–E–F♯).

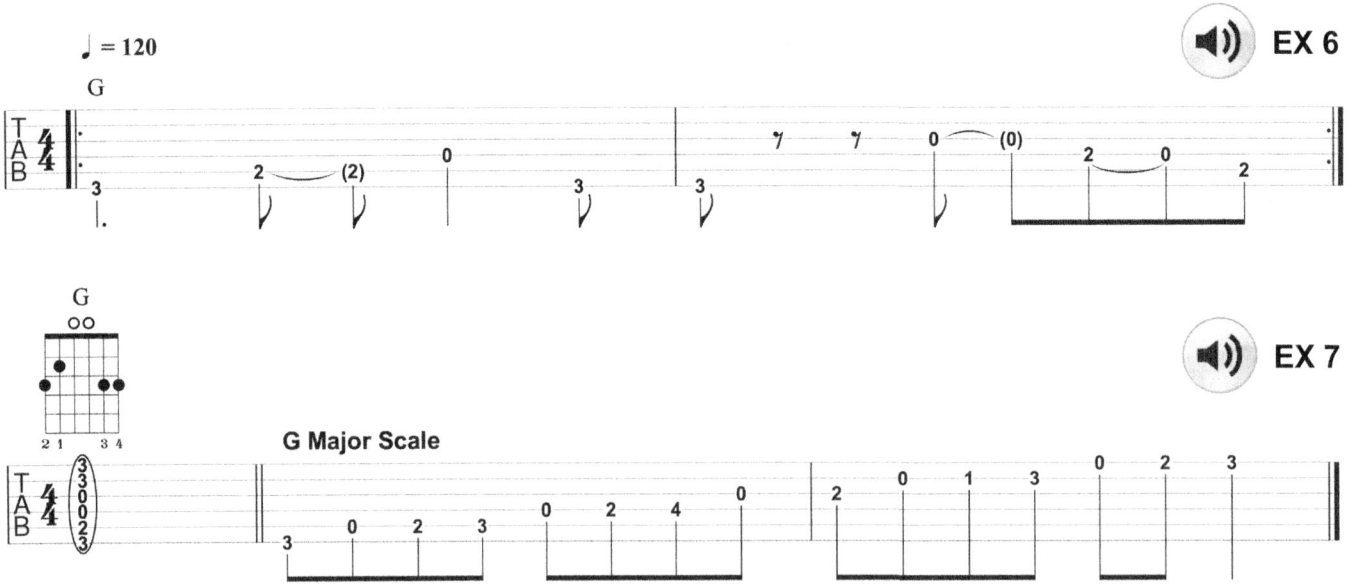

Let's imagine for a moment that the previous riff is an idea you came up with and now you're wondering how to turn it into a full-blown song. Well, with a riff like this one, the general inclination is to transpose it to the IV ("four") chord. Since G is our tonic, or I ("one") chord, the IV chord is C, the fourth note of the seven-note G major scale: **G**–A–B–**C**–D–E–F♯.

Finding the location of the IV chord, regardless of key, is pretty simple. If you're tonic, or root, note is located on string 6, then the IV chord is located on the same fret, just one string higher. If the tonic is on string 5, the IV chord can be found two frets, and one string, lower.

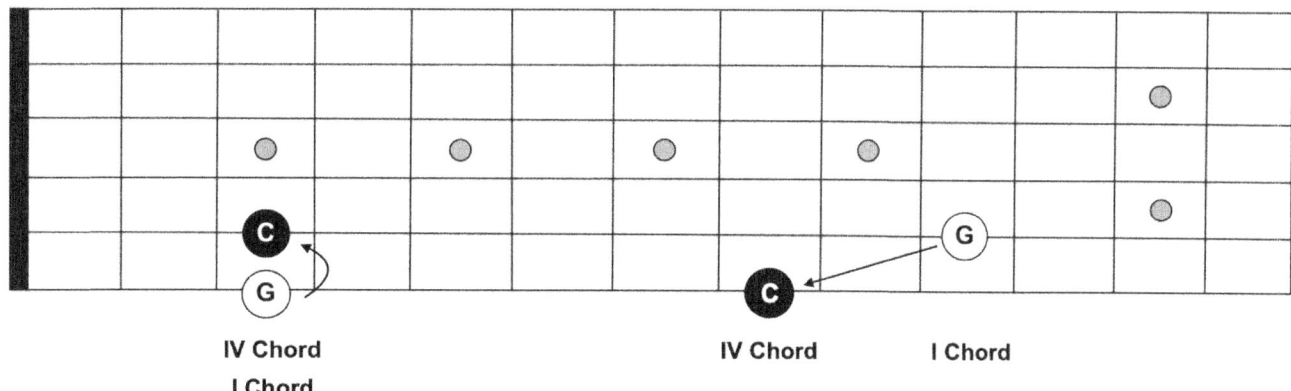

Now let's take our original riff and play all of the notes one string higher, like this:

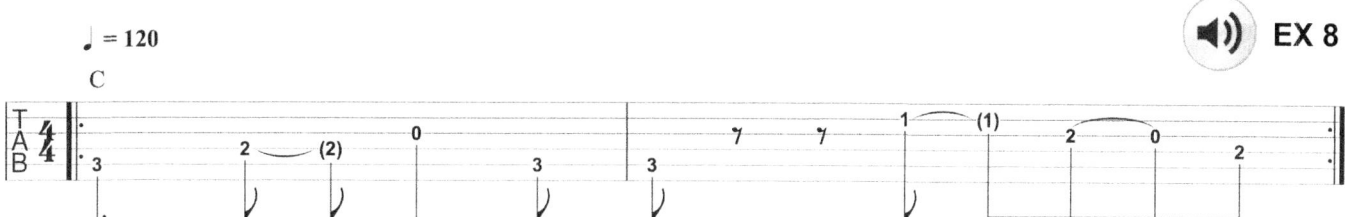

EX 8

Now the riff has been transposed to a new key, C major, and implies a new chord, C. This adds some harmonic movement to our riff. Instead of staying on a static G chord, we can move to the C riff and, by doing so, imply a G–C chord change:

EX 9

Now it's starting to sound like a song! If we transpose the riff one more time (use your ear for this—you don't have to know music theory), we can imply a third chord and then arrange the riffs to create a three-chord progression that can form the harmonic foundation of a verse, chorus, or bridge—or even a whole song! For example, let's move the C riff up a whole step to imply a D chord; that way, we can arrange the riffs to give our song a retro-rock vibe.

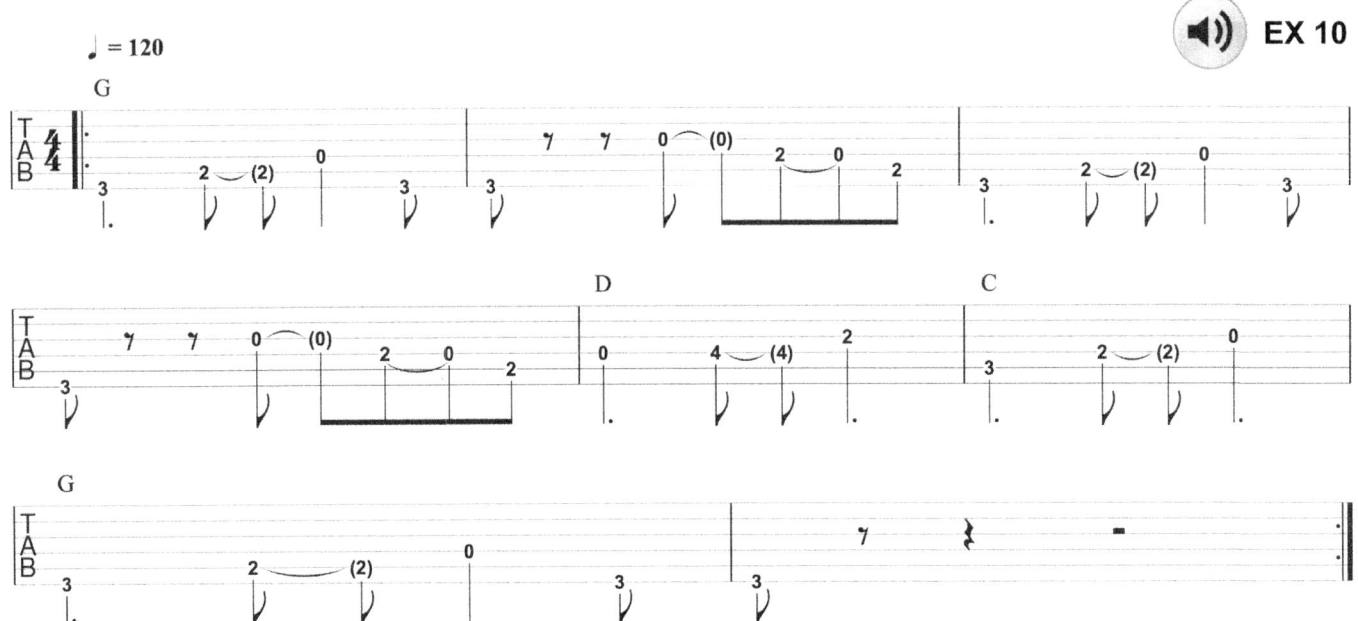

Notice in our implied progression, G–D–C–G, that the V (D) chord and IV (C) chord last only one bar each. To compensate for this, the D and C riffs have each been shortened by one bar. While the riffs certainly could've been left in their original two-bar form, I liked the energy and forward momentum of the one-bar phrases, so I decided to truncate the riffs. This is an important concept to consider when composing your own songs, because sometimes you need to alter your ideas to fit the progression (or song structure) you're hearing in your head. It's better to be flexible with your ideas than to try to fit a square peg into a round hole.

DOUBLE-STOP RIFFS
Now let's try another riff, this time focusing on double stops. For example, let's say you really like the sound of the sliding double stops below:

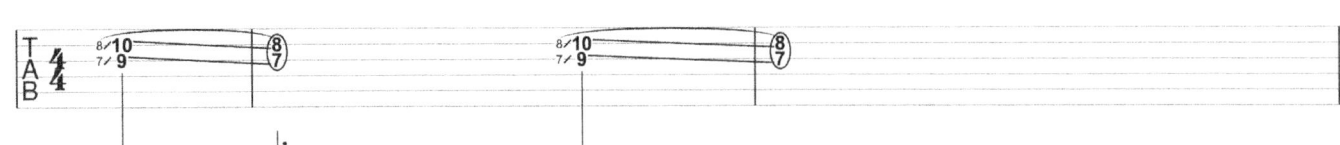

But how do you turn them into a riff? Well, like our previous riff, we need to expand on the idea a bit. To make it more musical, let's add some harmonic movement. But, first, we need to figure out what bass note(s) work with the double stops. Let's start with the first double stop—the one at fret 7. The two notes here are D (string 3) and G (string 2). Well, D and G are found in our trusty G chord, so let's try adding a G bass note to imply a G major chord, and also give the double stops some rhythm.

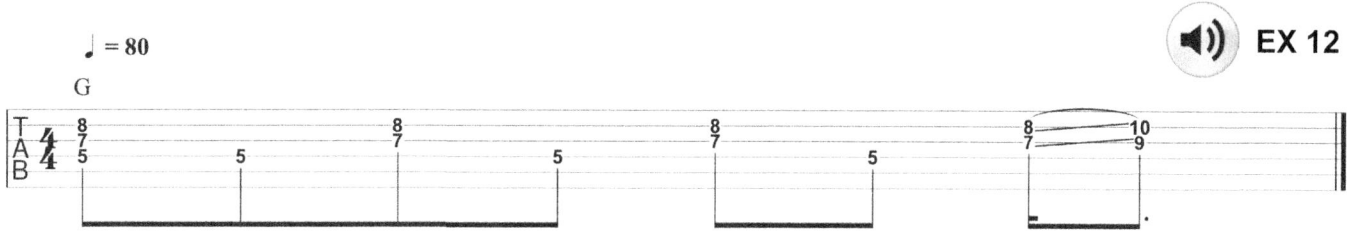

EX 12

That sounds pretty good. Now we need a second chord. Let's try moving to the V (D) chord, like we did in our previous riff. However, instead of continuing with the G/D double stop, let's add F♯, the D chord's 3rd, to really drive home the chord change.

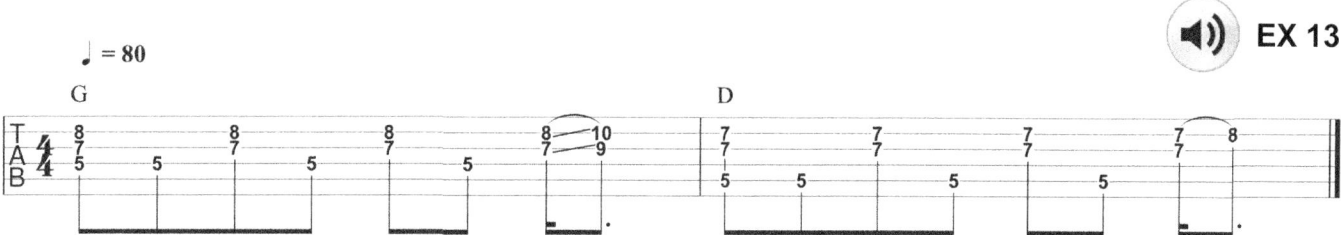

EX 13

I *really* like the sound of that! Now let's pick another chord to add to our two-chord progression. Let's try the relative minor, Em. We could incorporate the open low-E string to function as the Em chord's root, but I want to keep this chord in the same octave as the root of the D chord, so let's move two frets higher up the neck. Some finger adjustments will be required, but that's OK—sometimes that can result in some pretty great ideas. Let's give it a try…

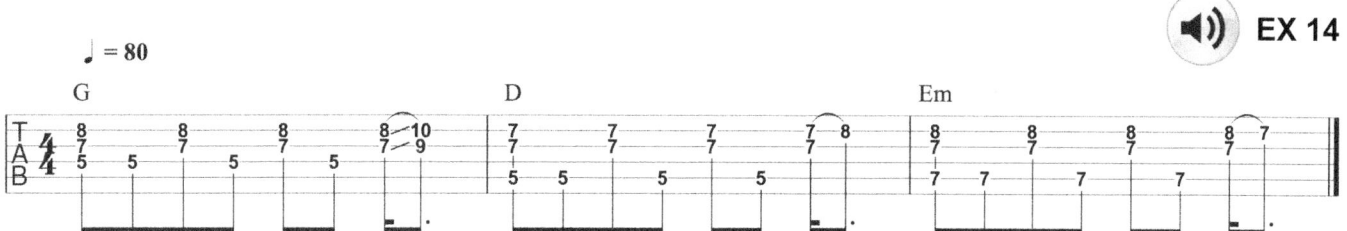

EX 14

That chord works nicely, too. Notice that, for the Em chord, the riff pulls off from G to F♯, rather than hammering from F♯ to G. This maneuver adds a little more interest to the melodic line that's starting to develop on string 2.

Now let's cap off our riff with one last chord. I think the IV chord, C, will work nicely in bar 4, giving us an implied G–D–Em–C (I–V–vi–IV) progression, a set of changes that can be heard in such songs as "When I Come Around" (Green Day), "Let It Be" (The Beatles), "Don't Stop Believin'" (Journey), and "Take on Me" (a-ha). Like the D chord, I really want to drive home this harmonic change, so let's drop down to 3rd position to play the C chord, which gives us the 3rd, E, on string 2. Also, I think this riff could use some more energy and forward momentum, so let's anticipate each change by one 16th note.

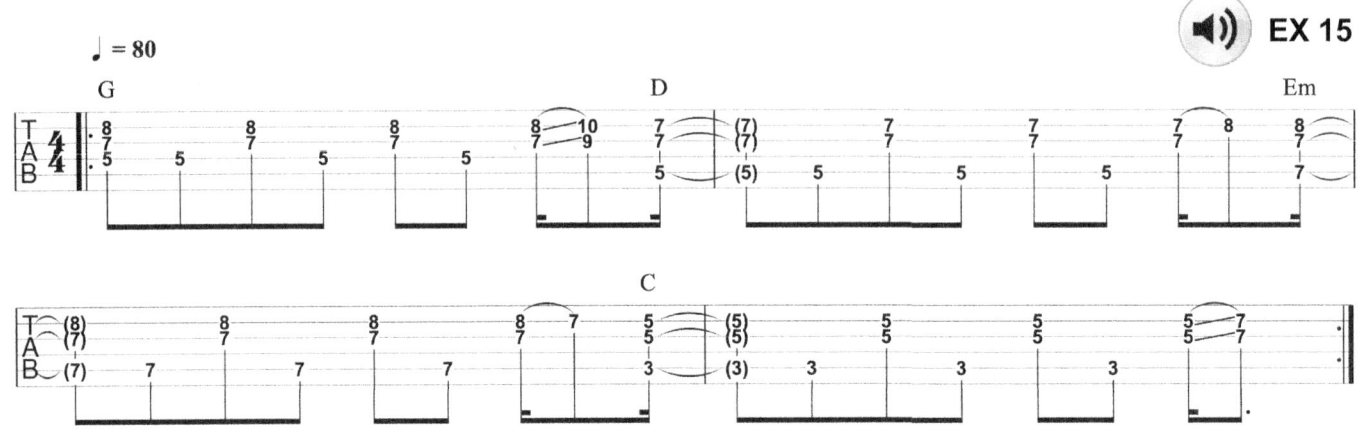

EX 15

There you have it—a catchy four-chord riff created from a simple double-stop idea. By now, I hope you're starting to see how small ideas can grow into bigger—and sometimes much cooler—song sketches. See if you can come up with some of your own.

CHAPTER 3: MELODY IS KING!

It doesn't matter if you can write the coolest riffs or create the most interesting chord progressions, if you can't bring melody into your music, you'll never reach your full potential as a composer or songwriter. And the reason is simple: melody is king!

In this chapter, we're going to look at how two- and three-note melodic ideas can bring inspiration to your songwriting sessions and, ultimately, become strong instrumental hooks in your compositions.

TWO-NOTE PHRASES

Let's begin with a simple two-note phrase. I've always liked the way the open high-E string sounds when it rings together with the C♯ note at fret 2 of string 2, so let's begin with those two notes.

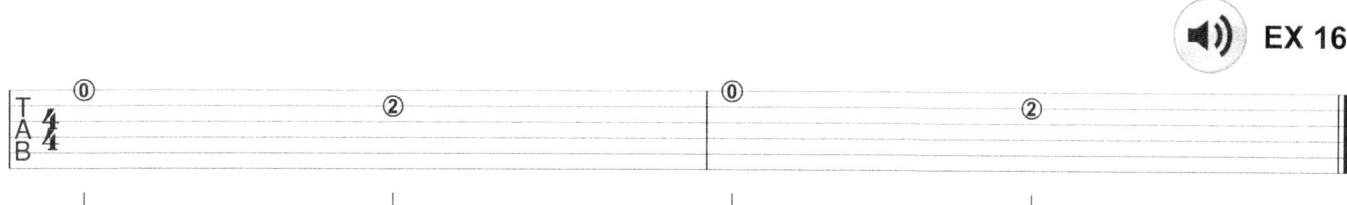

Right away, these notes having me thinking A chord (A–C♯–E). But, instead of using the full open-A voicing, let's just pluck the open A and then arpeggiate the E and C♯ notes. Although we're not strumming the full chord, we're still implying A major.

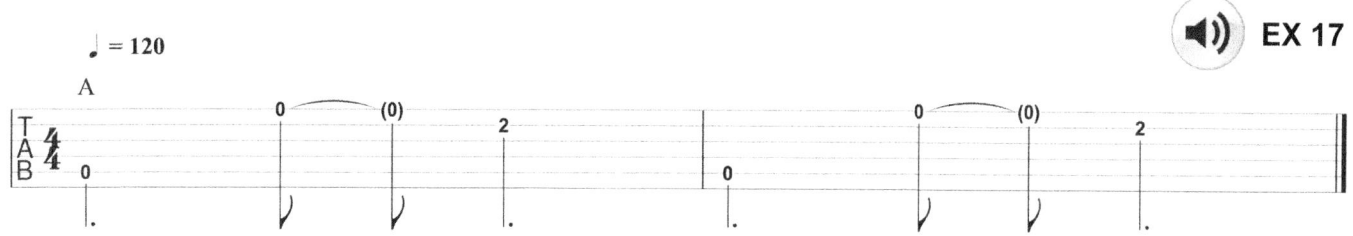

That's already starting to sound like a song! Now let's keep that melodic idea moving forward by changing our bass note to imply another chord. Since this riff already has a somewhat moody vibe—in spite of the major chord!—let's shift to the relative minor, F♯m.

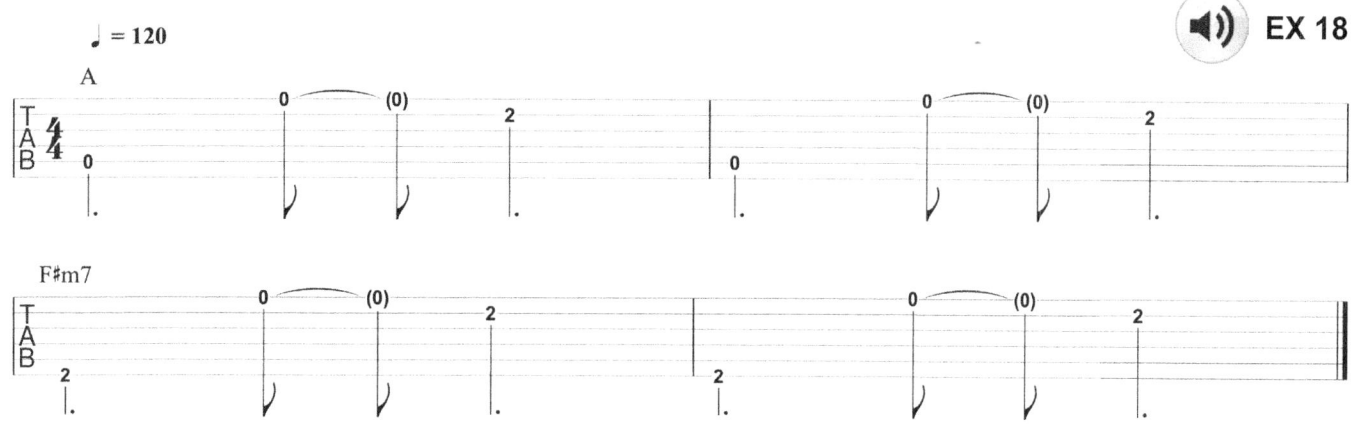

Once again, we're *implying* F♯m (F♯–A–C♯)—or, more specifically, F♯m7 (F♯–A–C♯–E)—rather than strumming the whole chord. Nonetheless, it still has the same effect: a discernable change in harmony.

15

What I like to do at this point is to experiment with different bass notes to hear how they sound against the first two root notes, A and F♯. For this type of riff, I'm a big proponent of open strings, so let's give the open low-E string a try:

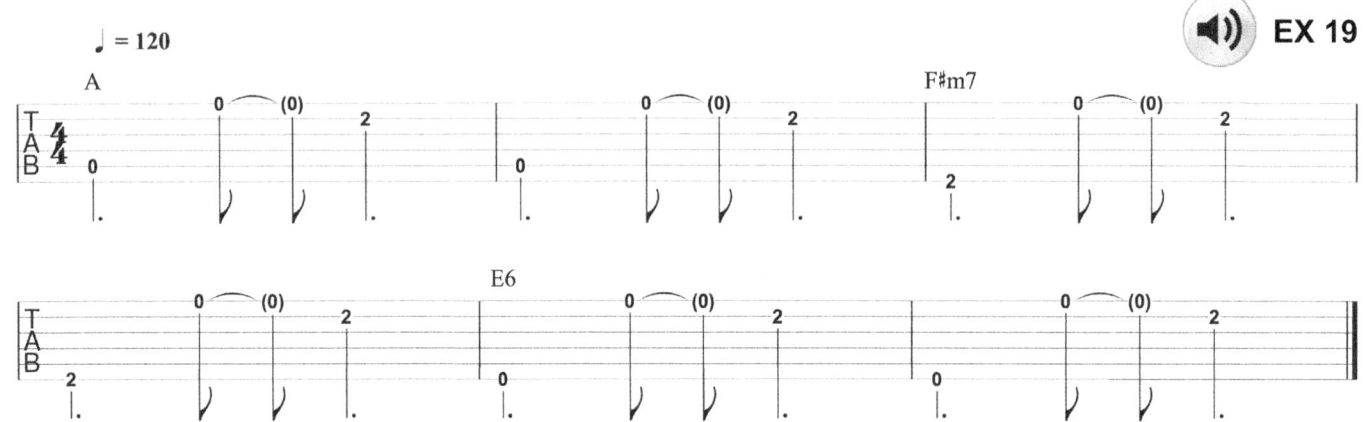

That low E works really well! This new harmony is somewhat ambiguous, but we'll call it E6 (E–G♯–B–C♯), which will give us a I–vi–V (A–F♯m–E) progression. Now let's add one more chord. A strong choice would be to go to the IV chord, D, giving us a I–vi–V–IV (A–F♯m–E–D) progression. Plus, we can utilize another open string, which is always a good thing! Let's see how that works…

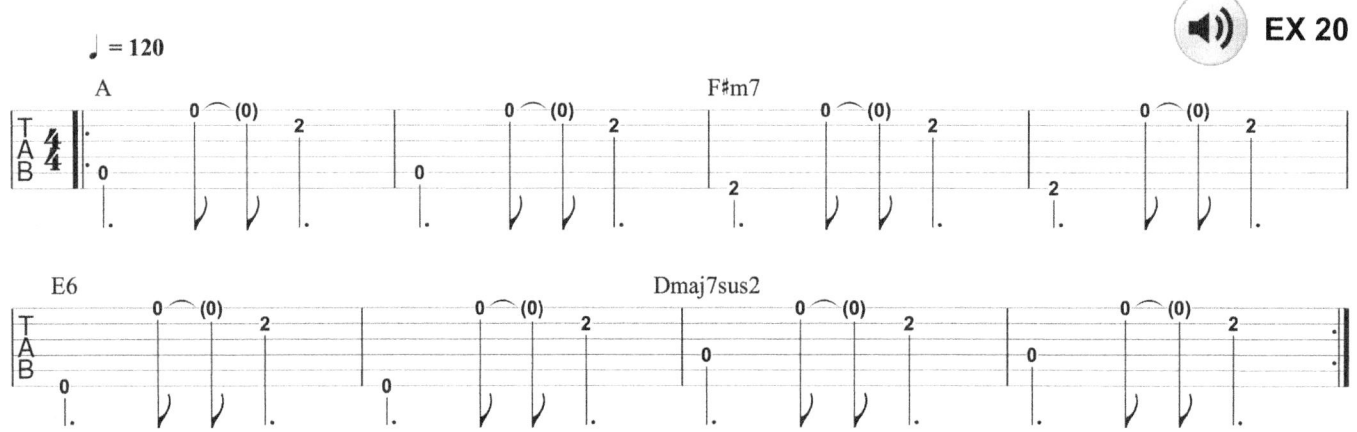

I think that'll do! Notice how the ringing bass notes enhance the simple two-note melody. And, despite some intimidating chord names, the riff's underlying progression is just a simple I–vi–V–IV in the key of A: A–F♯m–E–D.

THREE-NOTE PHRASES

Now let's work with a three-note melody and see what we can come up with. Let's try something further up the neck, like this:

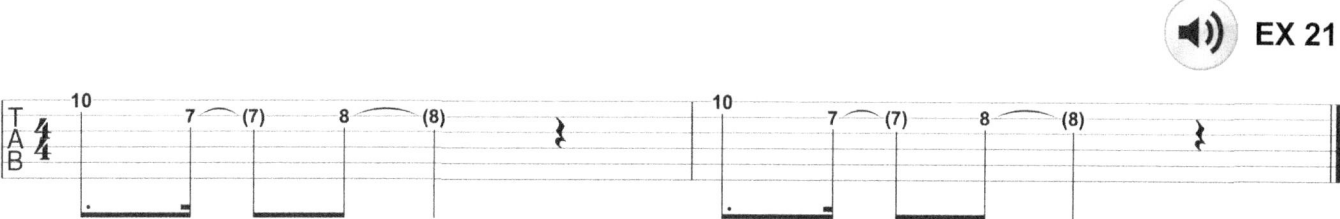

EX 21

I'm thinking a minor key would be best for this melody. Since we're working with the notes D, F#, and G, let's try incorporating a standard Em7 chord voicing to give the idea some harmonic heft.

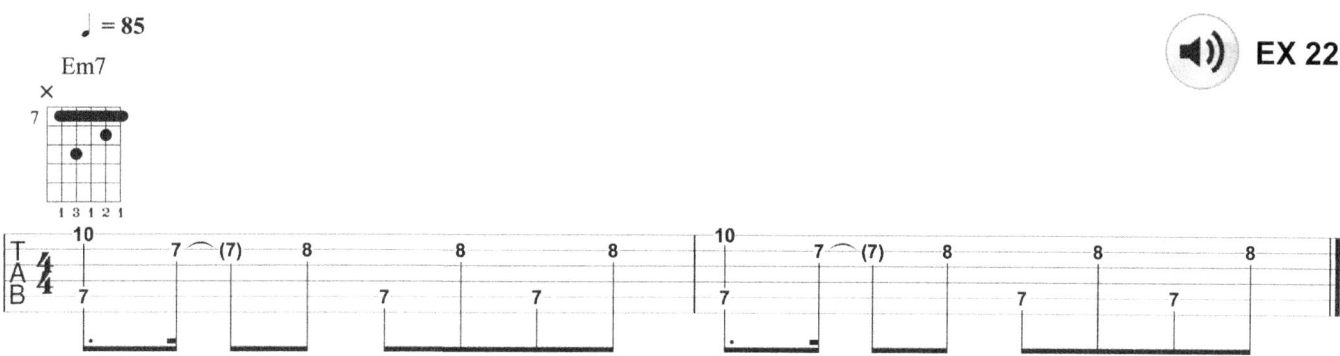

EX 22

I'm thinking a descending bass line would really give this melody some additional emotional content, so let's shift down a whole step to D while maintaining the three-note melody on top. This will imply a diatonic (i.e., in-key) D major chord. Fortunately, we can avoid some awkward stretches by incorporating the open D string!

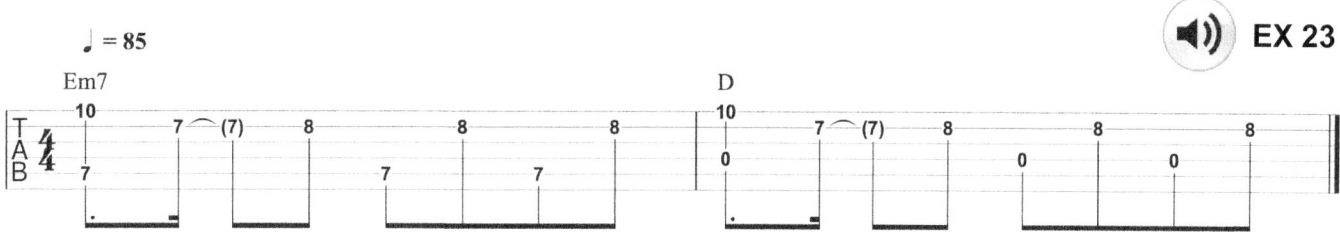

EX 23

I'm liking how that sounds. Now let's continue to descend the E minor scale (E–F#–G–A–B–C–D) by adding a C bass note. Unfortunately, there's no way to avoid awkward stretches for this chord. Hopefully, it won't give you too much trouble. One option is to wrap you thumb over the top of the fretboard to voice the C root note on string 6.

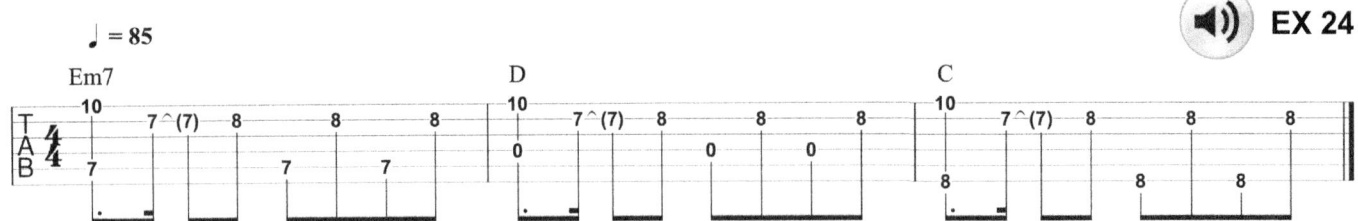

Now let's wrap up our melodic riff. Instead of adding a fourth chord at the top of measure 4, let's stay on the C chord for three more beats and then add the D chord to beat 4 to help transition back to the tonic chord, Em7.

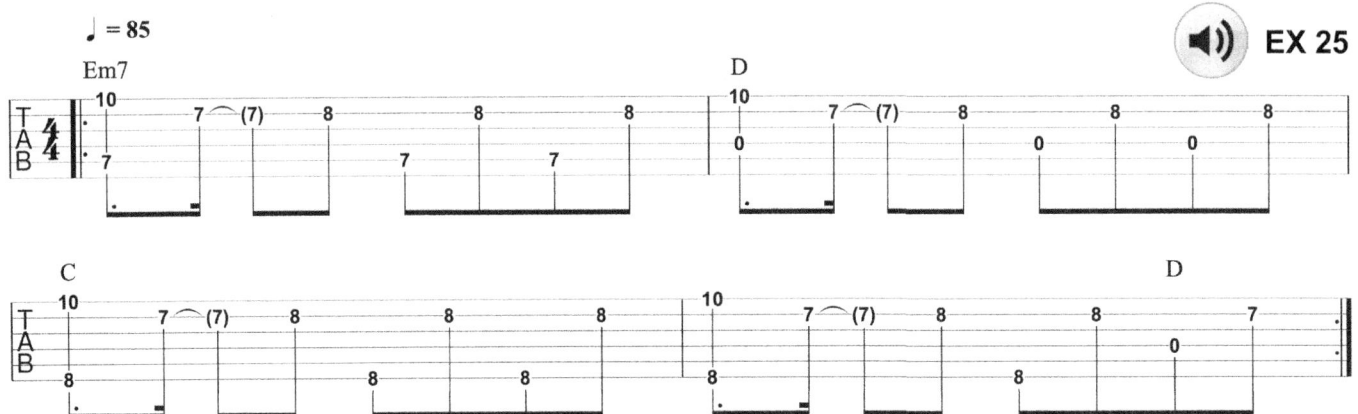

As the melody is maintained on top, the bass moves stepwise from E to D to C, implying a i–VII–VI (Em–D–C) progression in E minor.

CHAPTER 4: LET VIBE BE YOUR GUIDE

Vibe is a loosely defined term that encompasses your current mood, the mood of the people around you—perhaps in the writing room—and the general feeling you get from the room itself. Vibe can be both good and bad, or even somewhere in between. When applied to music, vibe generally refers to the feelings and emotions you get while listening to it. Does it make you happy? Sad? Energetic? Indifferent? Whatever the case may be, when writing a song, you want to let the vibe be your guide.

For example, let's say you come up with an uptempo riff with a driving rhythm and lots of powerful, palm-muted power chords. Are you going to write a ballad to that riff? Um, no. You're going to want to write an upbeat rock or metal song. Similarly, if you compose a gentle fingerpicking pattern, are you going to write a club banger? Well, of course not. What I'm trying to say is this: make sure your guitar parts fit the song, and your song (lyric, melody, etc.) fits your guitar parts. Of course, rules are meant to be broken, and that certainly applies to music and songwriting. However, there is an undeniable fact that certain chord progressions, as well as the style in which they're preformed, will convey the vibe of your song better than others.

UPTEMPO-BALLAD VIBE

Let's go over a few guitar ideas and discuss their qualities and the types of songs in which they'd feel most at home. For example, let's say you sit down with your guitar for a few minutes and come up with this:

EX 26

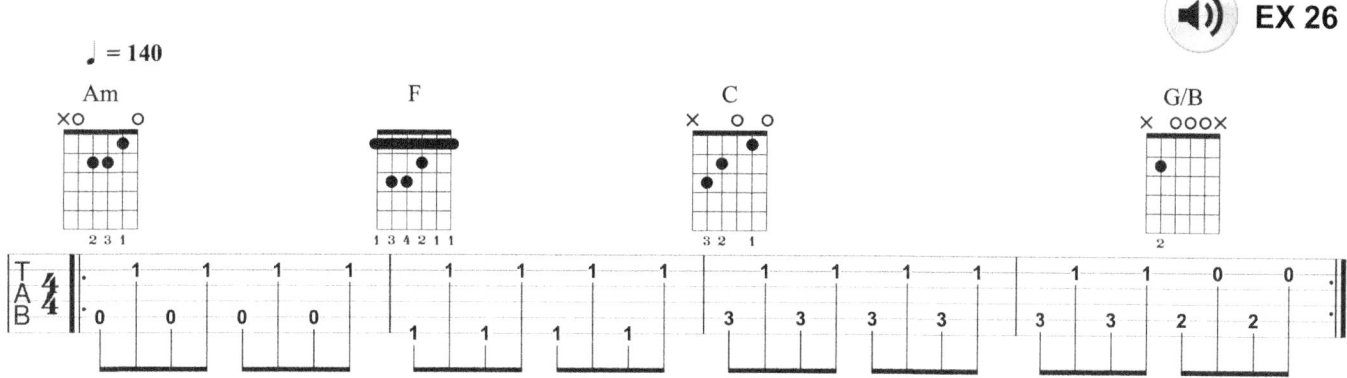

It's a pretty straightforward riff that plucks the root notes of an Am–F–C chord progression on the downbeats and the C note at fret 1 of string 2, which is common to each chord, on the upbeats. Then, at the end of bar 4, a G/B chord breaks up the melodic repetition and signals a return to the top of the riff.

How does this riff make you feel? What kind of vibe does it convey? For me, a couple of things stick out. First, the song is in a minor key, Am, so it has a slightly dark sound overall. Second, the driving eighth notes and frequent chord changes keep the song upbeat, despite the minor tonality. In my opinion, this riff would work well in an uptempo ballad in several genres—folk, rock, pop, etc.

RETRO VIBE

Let's try another one. The example below features a simple two-chord progression that is strummed in a mostly eighth-note rhythm. The defining characteristics of this guitar part are its two major 7th chords (Amaj7 and Dmaj7), rhythmic syncopations, and first-string melody in bar 4. To me, the major 7ths give this riff a '70s country vibe in the vein of Glen Campbell.

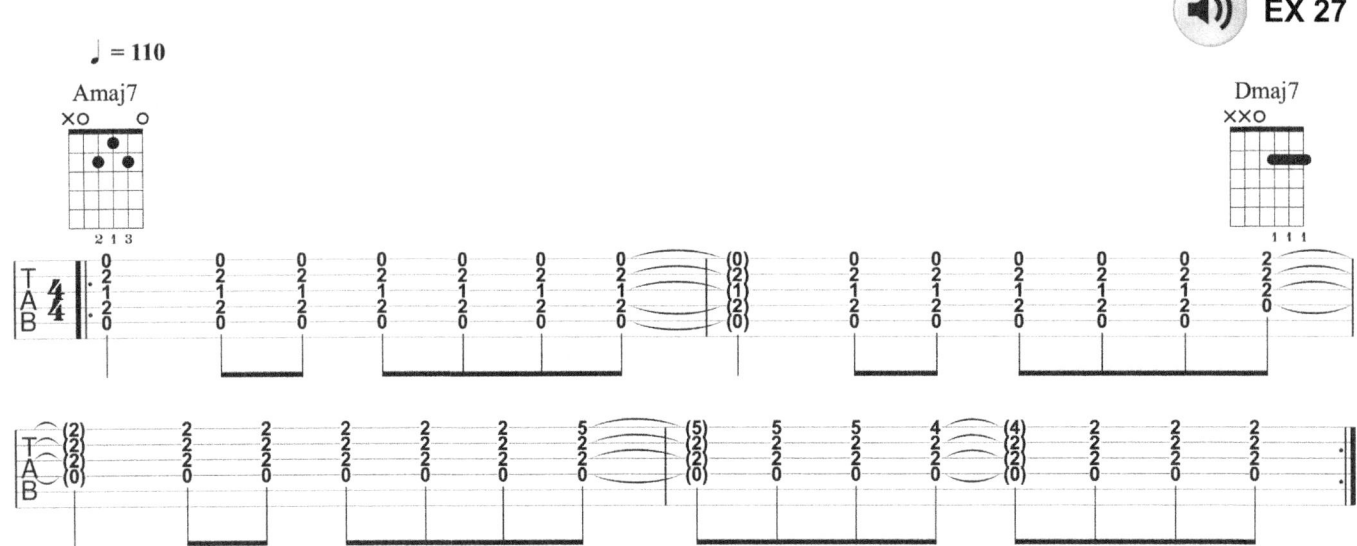

EX 27

Major 7th chords are common in genres like jazz, disco/funk, and fusion, but are infrequently heard on modern pop, rock, and country radio. That seems to be changing, however, as more and more artist search for "new" sounds. If the riff had relied on standard A and D triads, rather than major 7th voicings, the vibe would be much different. Sometimes the sound of a single chord (in this case, a major 7th) can dictate the entire feel of a song.

While this guitar riff certainly has a retro vibe, with a little modern production, it could sound right a home on pop radio—really, almost any genre. And, lyrically, there are a lot of avenues to venture down.

JOHN MAYER VIBE

Now let's take the opposite approach to songwriting on guitar, and start with a general concept, genre, and/or vibe and see if we can create a part for it. For example, let's say we want to create a guitar part that is acoustic-based, has a moderate tempo, and really grooves—like how John Mayer locks in with the snare drum. Well, the first thing I do is find a chord progression that I like and that has the right vibe.

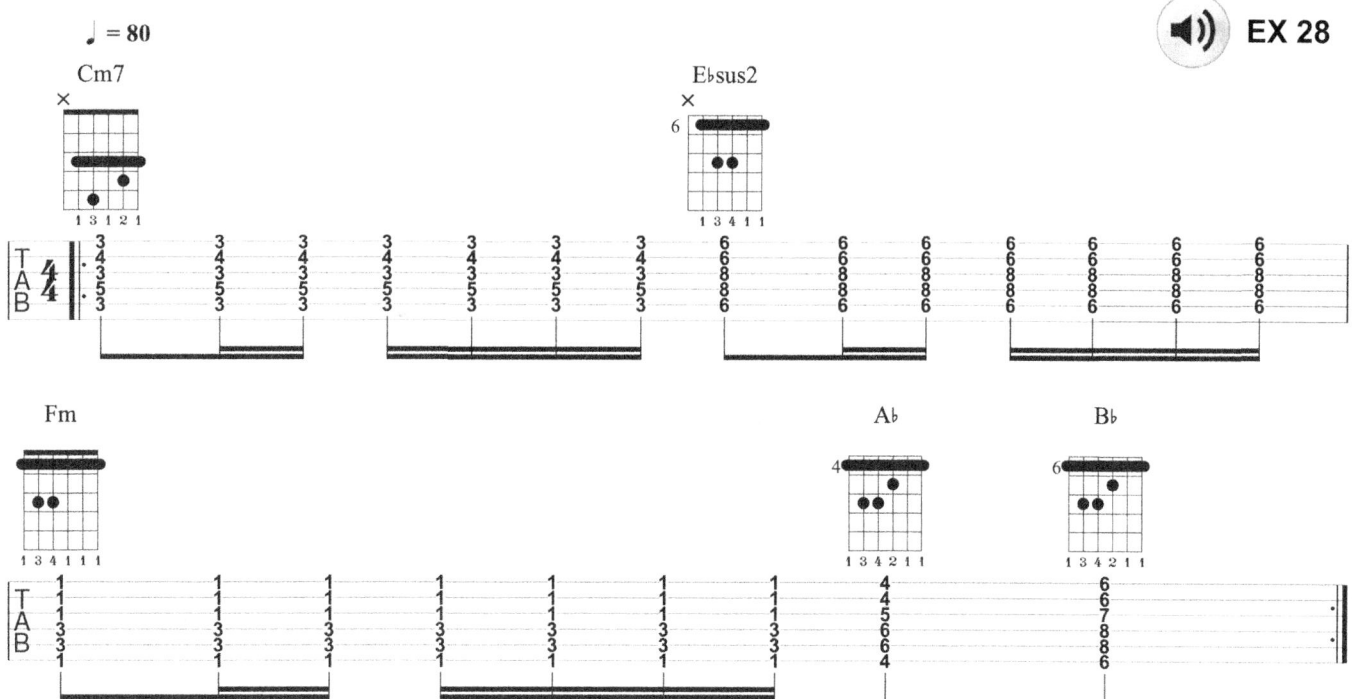

Now that I have the harmony, I need to make it groove like John Mayer. To do this, I'm going to arpeggiate the chords with my fingers on beats 1 and 3 and then slap my fingers onto the strings on beats 2 and 4 in a percussive manner to mimic the snare drum, like this:

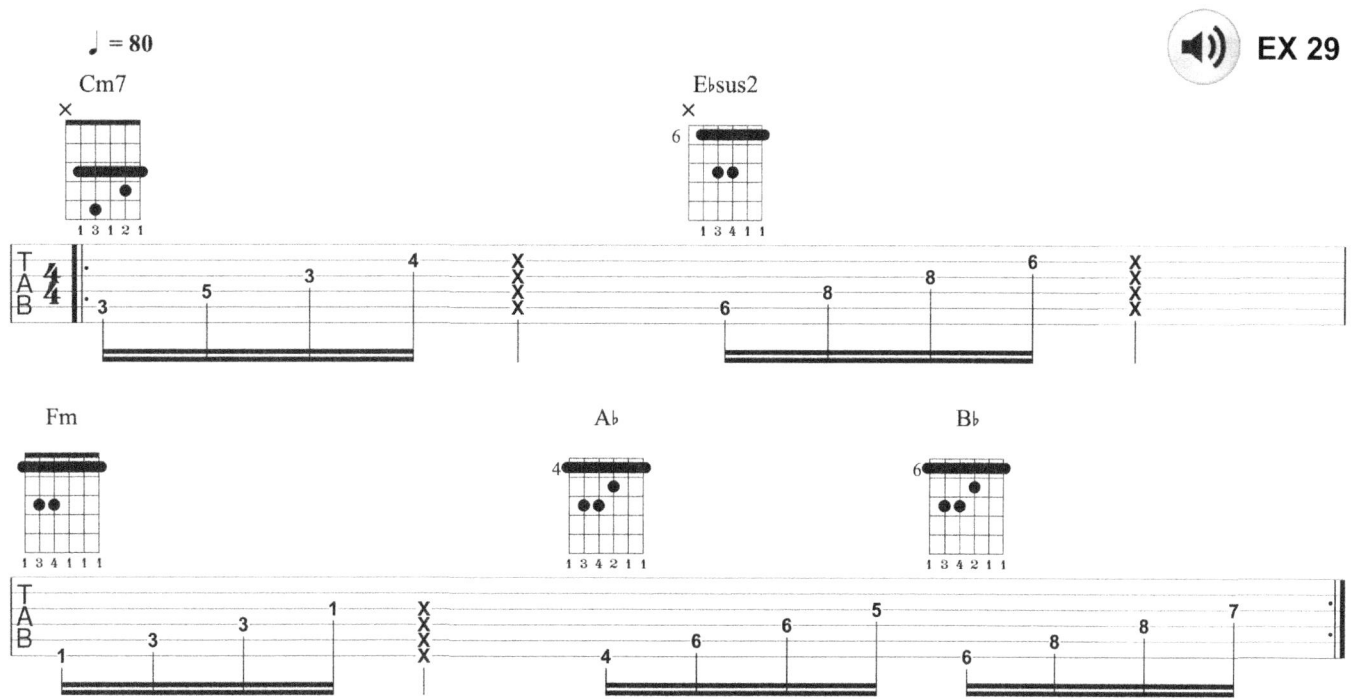

Now that sounds like John Mayer! Although the tempo is only 80 beats per minute (BPM), the 16th-note subdivision gives the impression that the pace is much faster than it really is. Notice, too, how the pick-hand slaps on beats 2 and 4 really help the part groove, even without the aid of a drummer or bass player. Mission accomplished!

DISCO/FUNK VIBE

Let's wrap up this chapter with one more example. This time, let's create an uptempo guitar part that has a late '70s/early '80s disco/funk vibe—you know, something that Nile Rodgers would play on a Dua Lipa track. Like our previous example, let's start by finding a chord progression that works for this vibe:

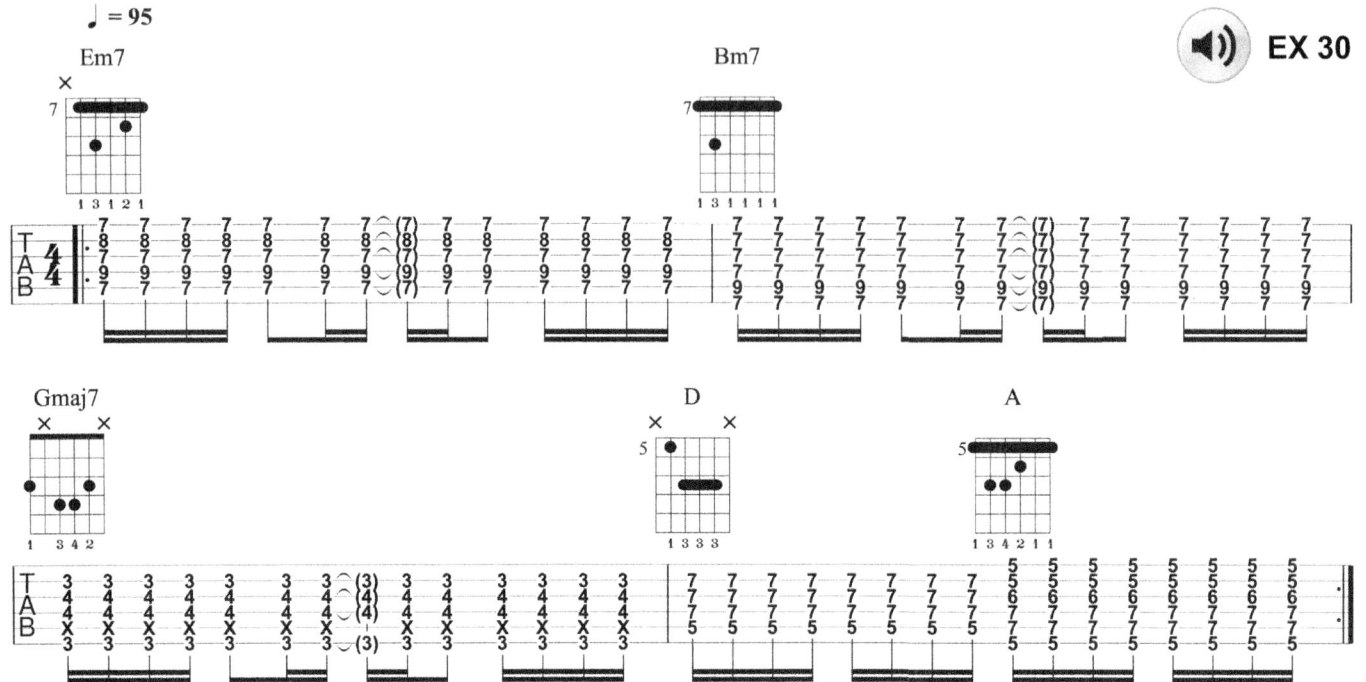

Although played in a pretty straightforward rhythm, you can already start to feel the funk because of the harmonic vibe of these chord changes. Now let's add some funk flair to the chords to give the part the full Nile Rodgers treatment.

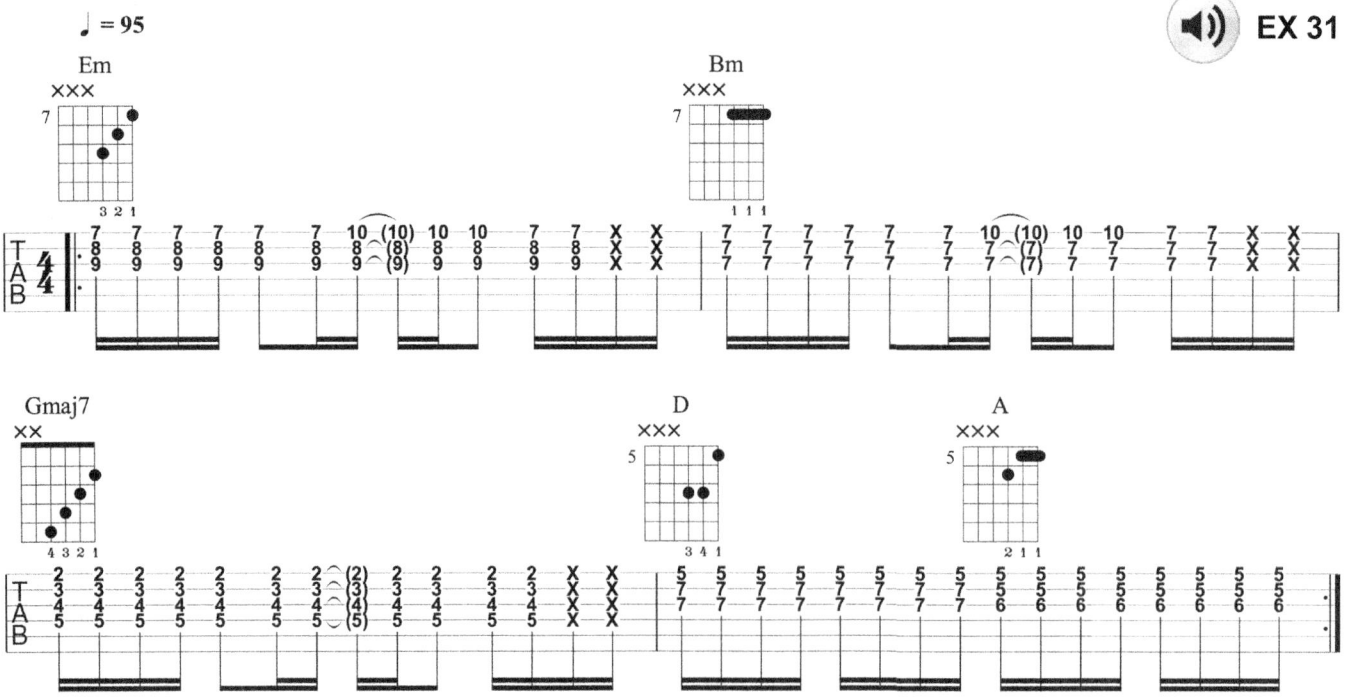

Now that's a riff you can hear Dua Lipa singing over! When it comes to creative songwriting on guitar, just remember to let vibe be your guide.

SECTION 2: SPICING UP BLAND CHORDS

One thing all guitar players—actually, all *musicians*—are guilty of is recycling chord progressions. We get accustomed to hearing the bass notes move a certain way and certain chord qualities (major, minor, etc.) appearing in the same spots of our progressions. The reason for this is mainly—or at least partly—due to the fact that we're used to hearing *diatonic* progressions; that is, progressions whose chords all belong to the same chord family, or key.

Diatonic progressions are what we overwhelming hear in popular music and on the radio, so it only makes sense for us to feel a connection to these types of progressions. After all, we tend to gravitate toward what is familiar. In the next few chapters, we're going to go over several ways you can spice up your dull and uninspired chord progressions.

CHAPTER 5: USING "UNEXPECTED" CHORDS

One way to really spice up a bland chord progression is to introduce one or two "unexpected" chords—chords that the listener is not anticipating. These types of chord substitutions typically—but not always—involve *non-diatonic* chords—chords that fall outside of the parent key of the progression. This can add harmonic excitement to an otherwise predictable set of chord changes.

Below is a set of changes you've probably played a thousand times. It's a I–IV–vi–V (E–A–C#m–B) in the key of E but with voicings that allow the top strings to ring freely.

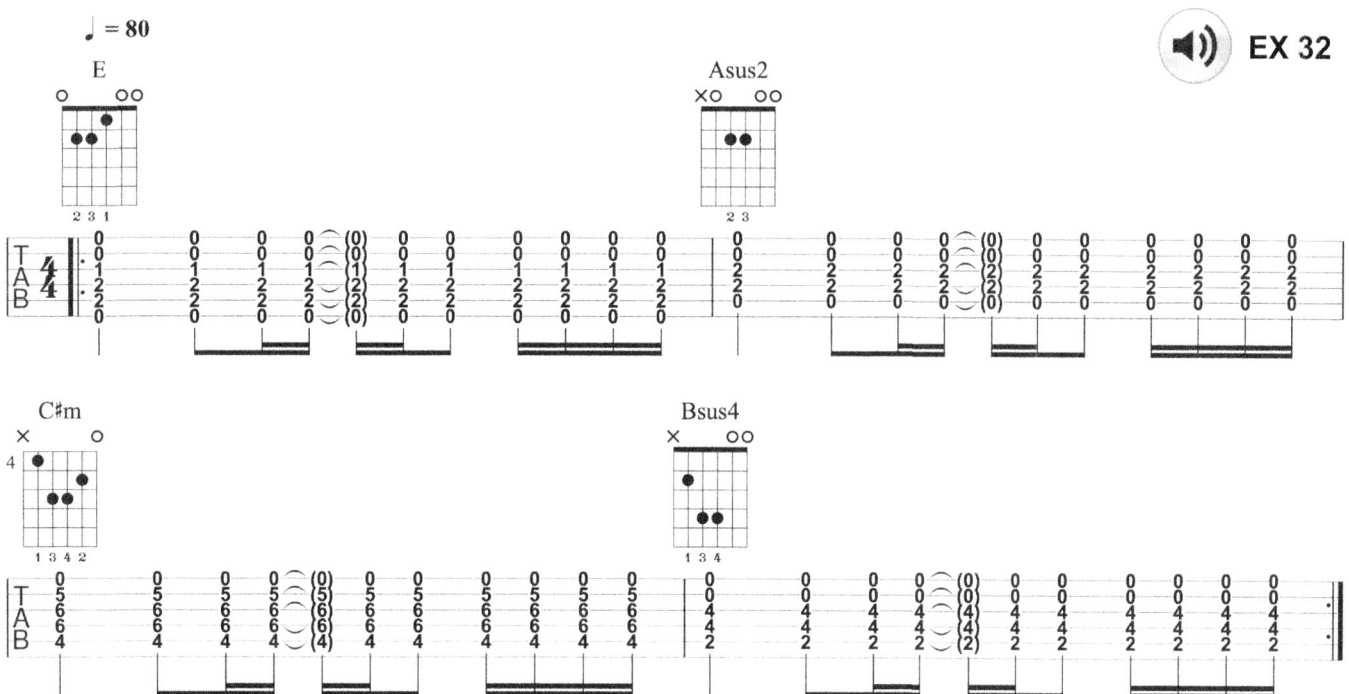

THE MINOR III CHORD

Honestly, the chords sound fine as is—maybe even worthy of a song. However, why not do a little experimentation to see if you can take the progression to the next level? For example, you could stay in the same key (E) but use a chord that often gets overshadowed by others: the III ("three") chord. In the key of E, the III chord is G♯m (technically, a iii [minor] chord). Let's try substituting G♯m for the IV chord, A, and hear how it sounds.

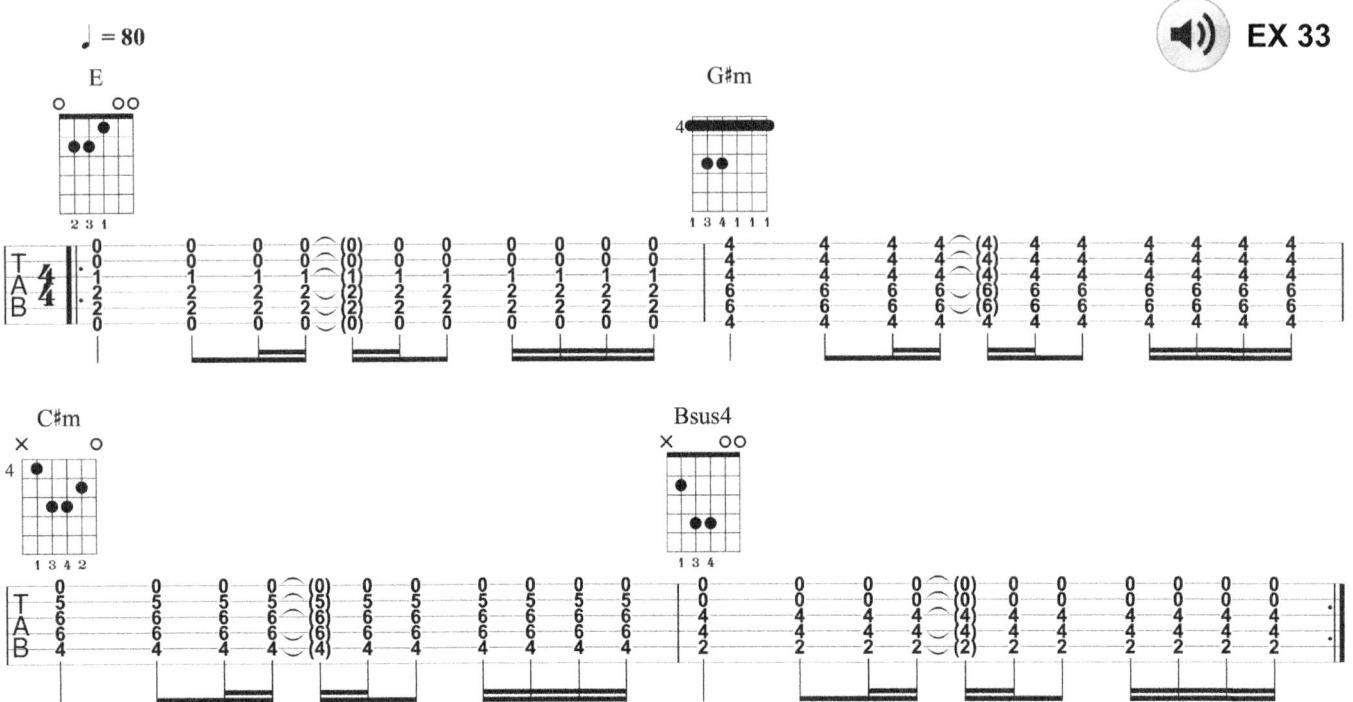

The G♯m chord sounds pretty darn good. Plus, your ear wasn't expecting the progression to go there. You could incorporate open strings into the G♯m change, as well:

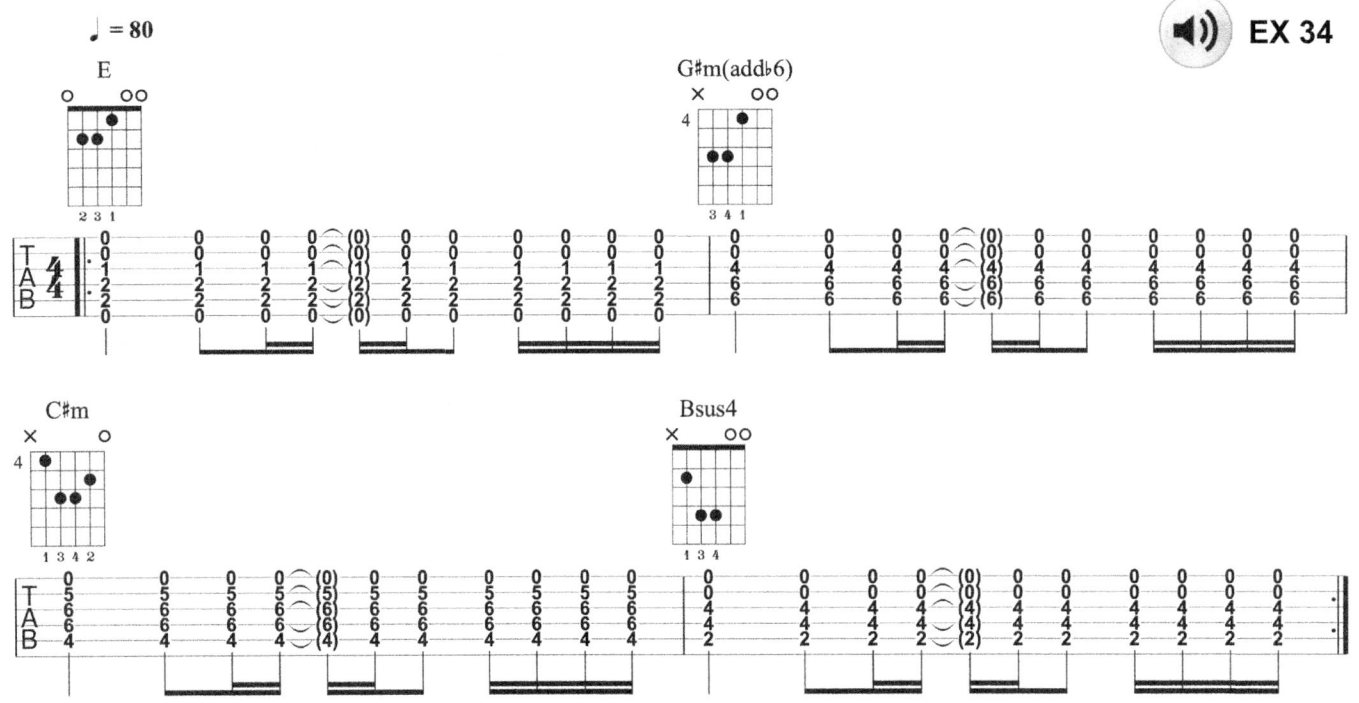

NON-DIATONIC CHORDS

Our first example was a diatonic progression—because all of the chords belong to the same key, E—but now let's take a look at a few *non*-diatonic chords that can be used to spice up your changes. For example, let's say you've come up with the following progression:

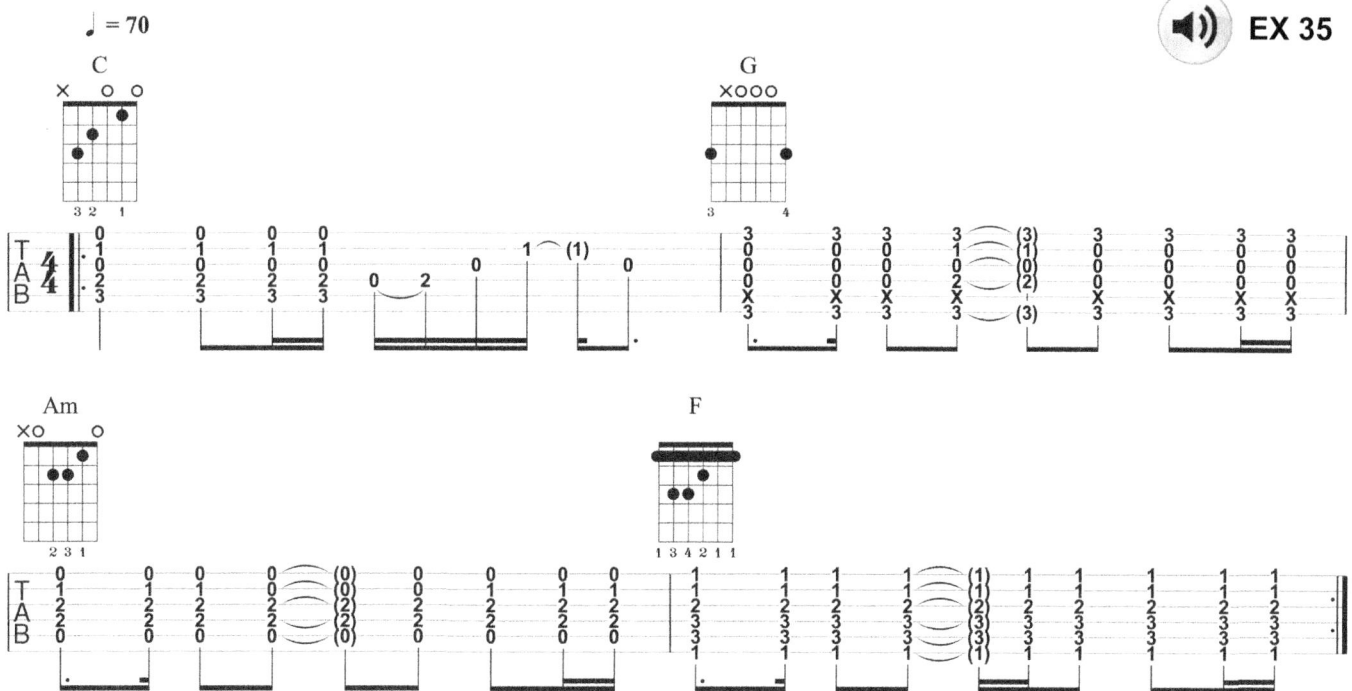

While the chords embellishments in bars 1–3 help to add more interest to the progression, the diatonic C–G–Am–F (I–V–vi–IV) changes could use some spice, harmonically, so let's add a substitution that's easy to implement and has been used in some rather notable songs, including "Blackbird" (The Beatles), "Don't Look Back in Anger" (Oasis), and "Wake Me Up When September Ends" (Green Day), to name just a few.

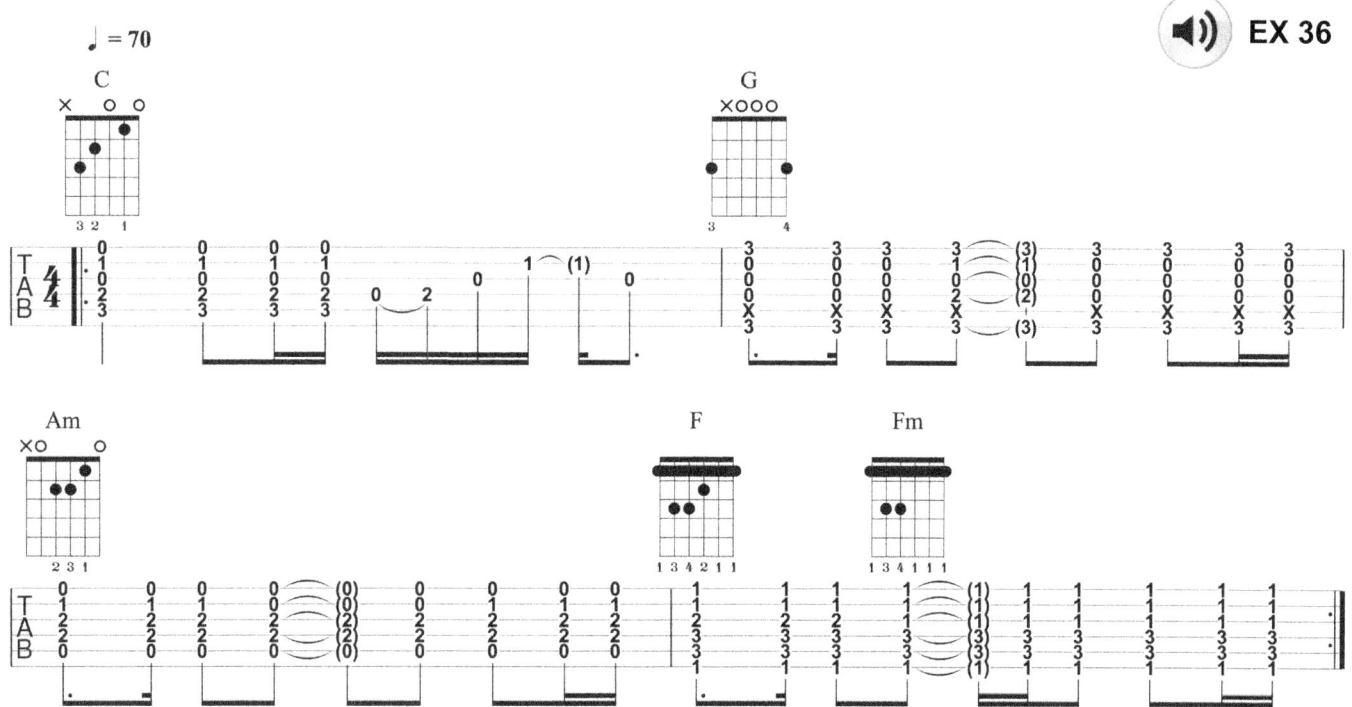

25

All we did to add a little more harmonic character to our progression was move from the diatonic IV chord, F, to its parallel minor, Fm, by simply removing our middle finger from string 3. Moving from the major IV to the minor iv chord—in any key—is a surefire way to add some harmonic spice to your progression.

Now let's look at another non-diatonic chord substitution that can be used to liven up your chord changes. In our first example of this chapter, we discussed substituting the minor iii chord to add interest to progressions. Now let's hear how it sounds if we add the *major* III chord to an otherwise set of diatonic chords. First, let's play the progression, G–Bm–C–D (I–iii–IV–V), with the diatonic minor iii chord:

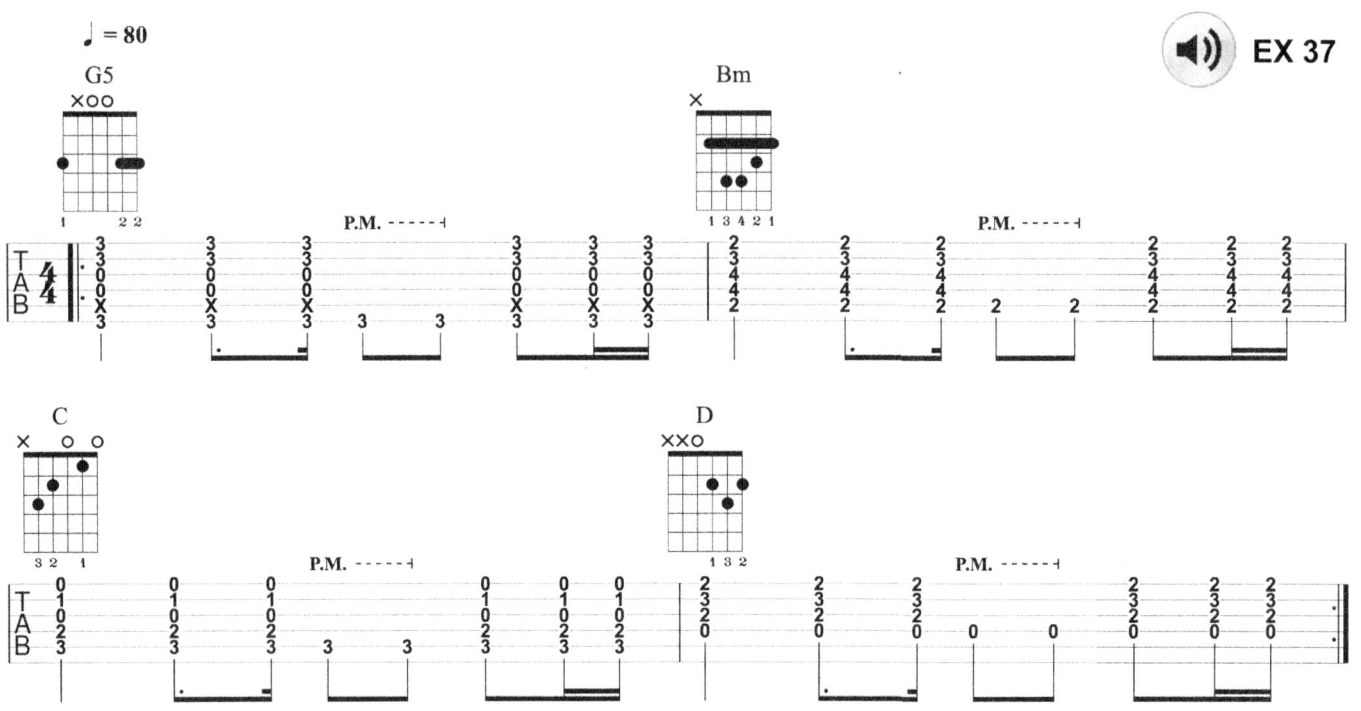

Now let's substitute the major III chord, B, for the minor iii chord, Bm:

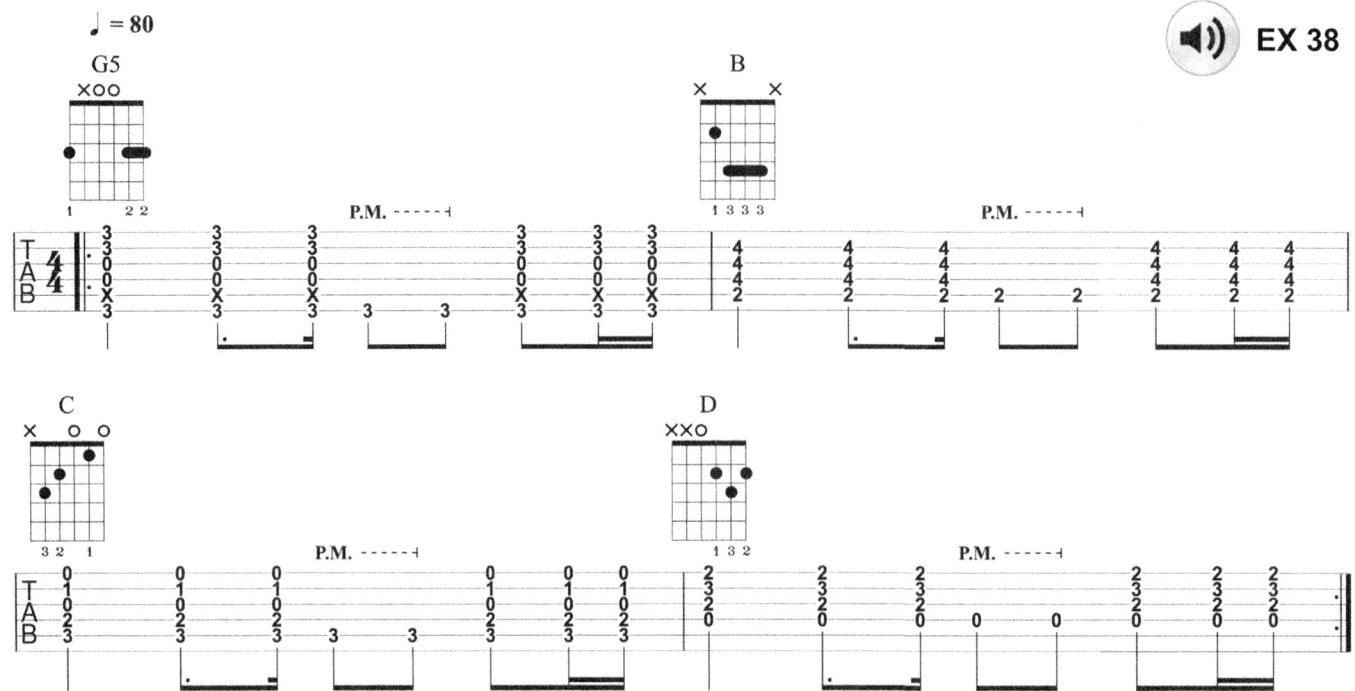

Sounds good, doesn't it? At the very least, it piques your interest. This non-diatonic chord—major III in a major progression (in our case, a B chord in a G major progression)—can be heard in songs like "Creep" (Radiohead) and "Imagine" (John Lennon). The major III chord also sounds good when voiced as a dominant 7th chord, like this:

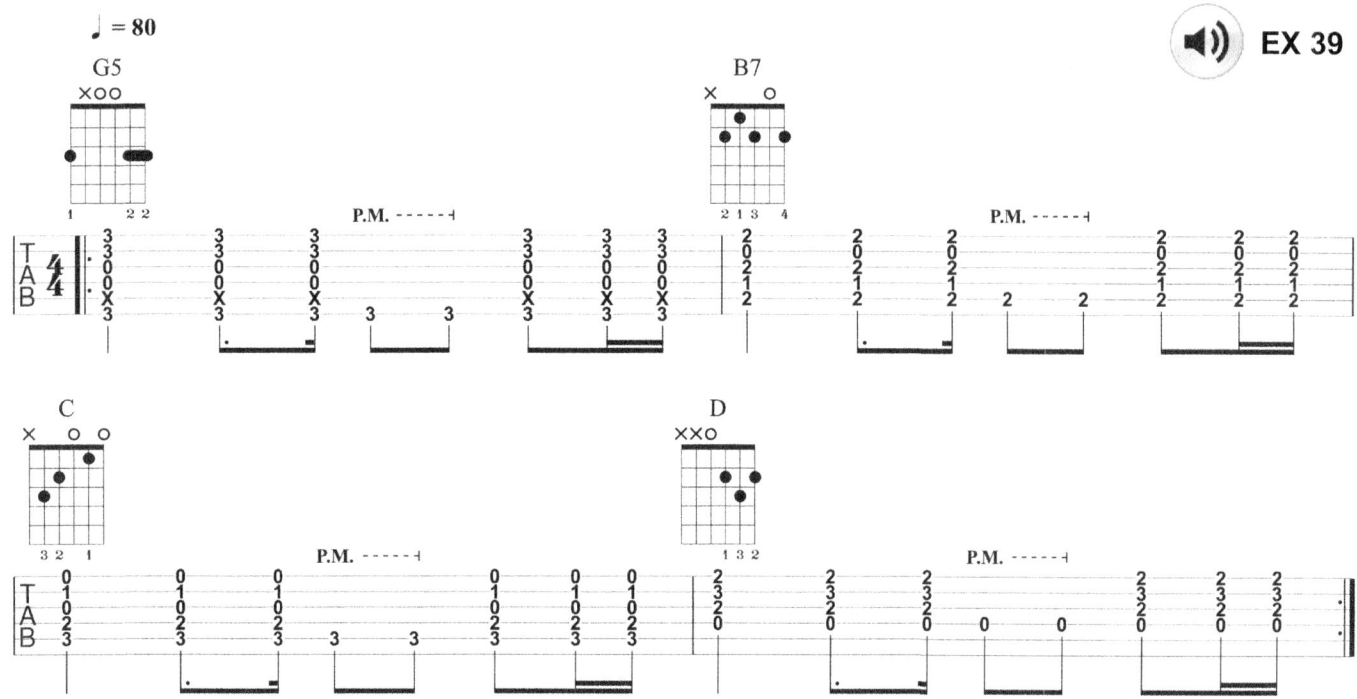

This chord change, I–III7 (G–B7), can be heard in Tim McGraw's "Live Like You Were Dying," where it's used to emphasize the lyric "…and I *spoke* sweeter…" The dominant 7th chord gives a feeling of uplift, which works really well in the context of this song about living life to the fullest.

Like the major-key progressions in this chapter, major chords can be substituted for minor ones in *minor* progressions, as well. For example, let's say we're working on a diatonic minor progression like this one:

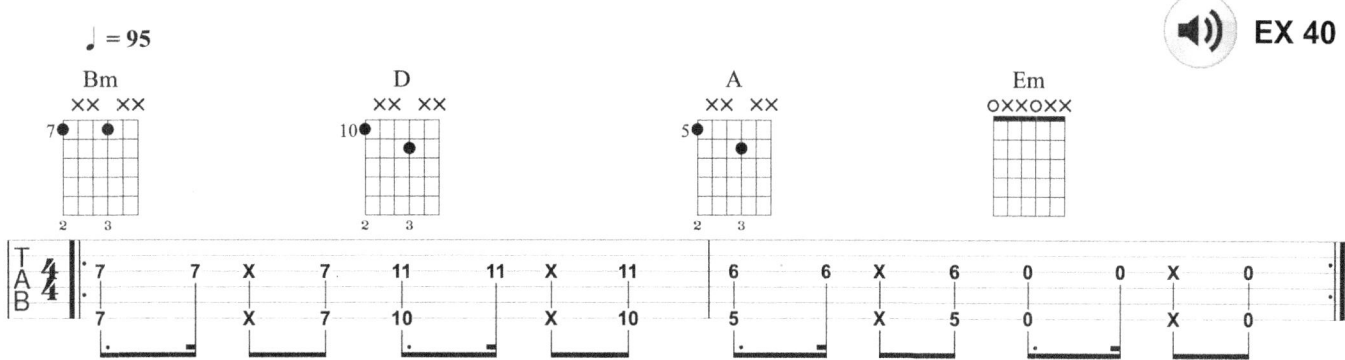

Although it has an equal number of major (D and A) and minor (Bm and Em) chords, this progression (i–III–VII–iv in B minor) has a distinctly minor tonality. Sometimes, however, minor progressions can sound just a bit too dark for the song we're trying to create, and a major progression would be just too bright- and happy-sounding. One solution to this problem is substitute a major chord for one of the minor ones. Since Bm is the tonic chord, we'll need to keep that one intact. However, we *can* replace the Em chord with E major. Let's give that a try:

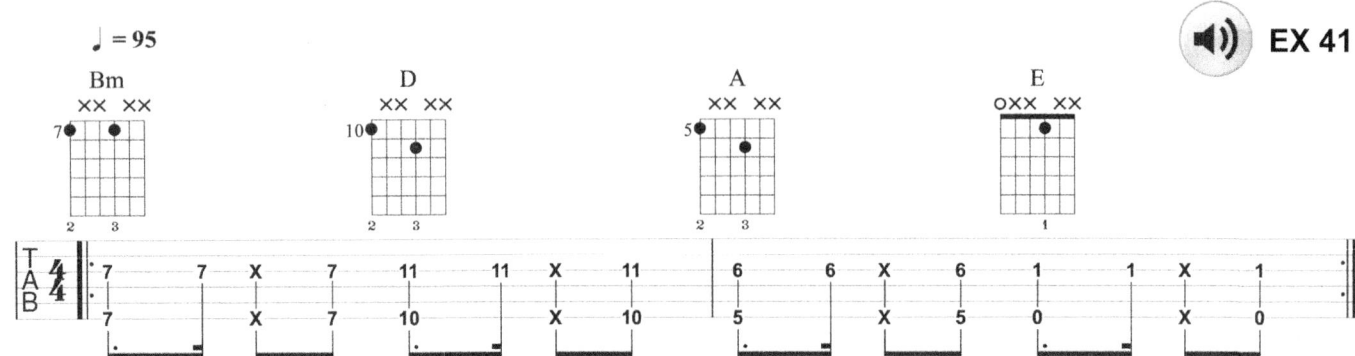

Notice that, by making this slight adjustment, turning the iv chord from minor (Em) to major (E), the mood of the progression lightens up a bit while still maintaining its melancholic, minor-key sound. In other words, it's still dark, but not *too* dark.

Without getting too deep into the music-theory weeds, what we've done here is we've derived our chords from the B Dorian mode (B–C#–D–E–F#–G#–A), a slightly brighter minor scale, rather than the more traditional—and darker—B minor (Aeolian) scale (B–C#–D–E–F#–G–A). So, if you're writing a minor-key song and it's sounding too sad or dark, then try replacing the minor iv chord with its parallel major—the major chord sharing the same root. Heck, you could experiment with replacing *any* of the minor chords with their major counterpart, not just the iv chord.

CHAPTER 6: CHORD EMBELLISHMENT

Chord embellishment, or ornamentation, is one of the quickest and easiest ways to turn a bland chord progression into something that sounds entirely new and exciting. *Chord embellishment* involves adding or subtracting notes from common chord voicings to add color and movement, which helps to captivate the attention of your listeners and spice up otherwise bland, predictable progressions. Chord embellishments can be applied to virtually any chord and can range from simple open-chord ornamentation to rather complex embellishment like Jimi Hendrix's "Little Wing." Let's take a look at a few relatively easy concepts that you can apply to your own chord progressions to give them extra life.

OPEN-CHORD ORNAMENTATION

Let's start with some common open-chord ornamentation. Here's a straightforward G–Cadd9–G–D progression (I–IV–I–V in the key of G) with no embellishment:

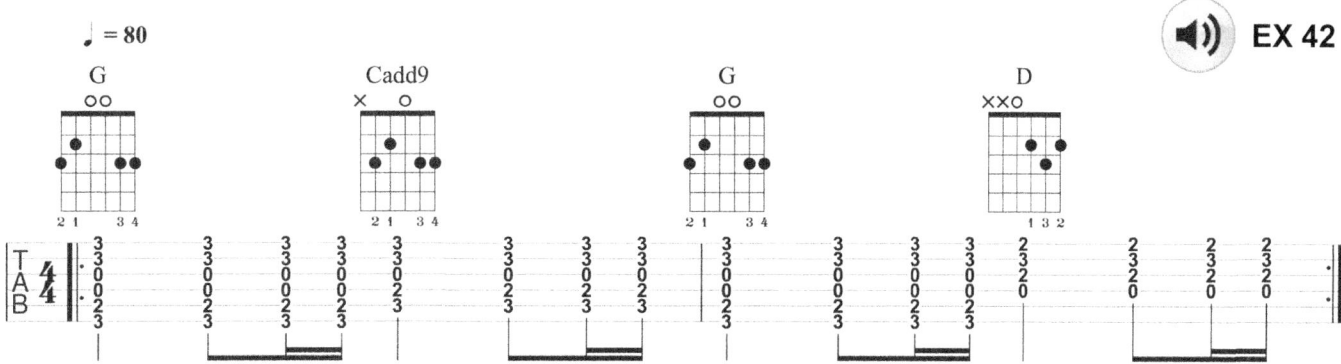

Now let's use some common methods for embellishing each chord. For the G and Cadd9 chords, the 3rds (B and E, respectively) are approached from a whole-step below (the open A and D strings) and followed by open strings that are part of their respective chords. At the end of bar 2, the D chord gets in on the action with a quick pull-off from G to F♯ on string 1, briefly implying a Dsus4 chord.

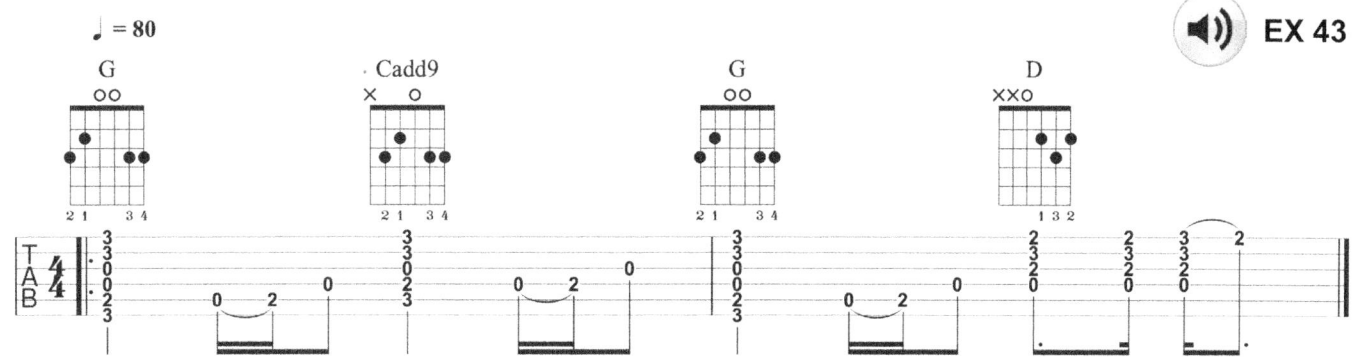

Notice how much more interesting the second example is compared to the first. Those few, small embellishments make a big difference in the overall sound and energy of the progression. Try adding embellishment to some of your favorite open-chord progressions, using your ears as a guide.

Let's stay in open position and embellish the chords of another common progression, C–F–Am–G–F (I–IV–vi–V–IV in the key of C). The example on the next page, a moderately slow 6/8 waltz, is played with no embellishment.

29

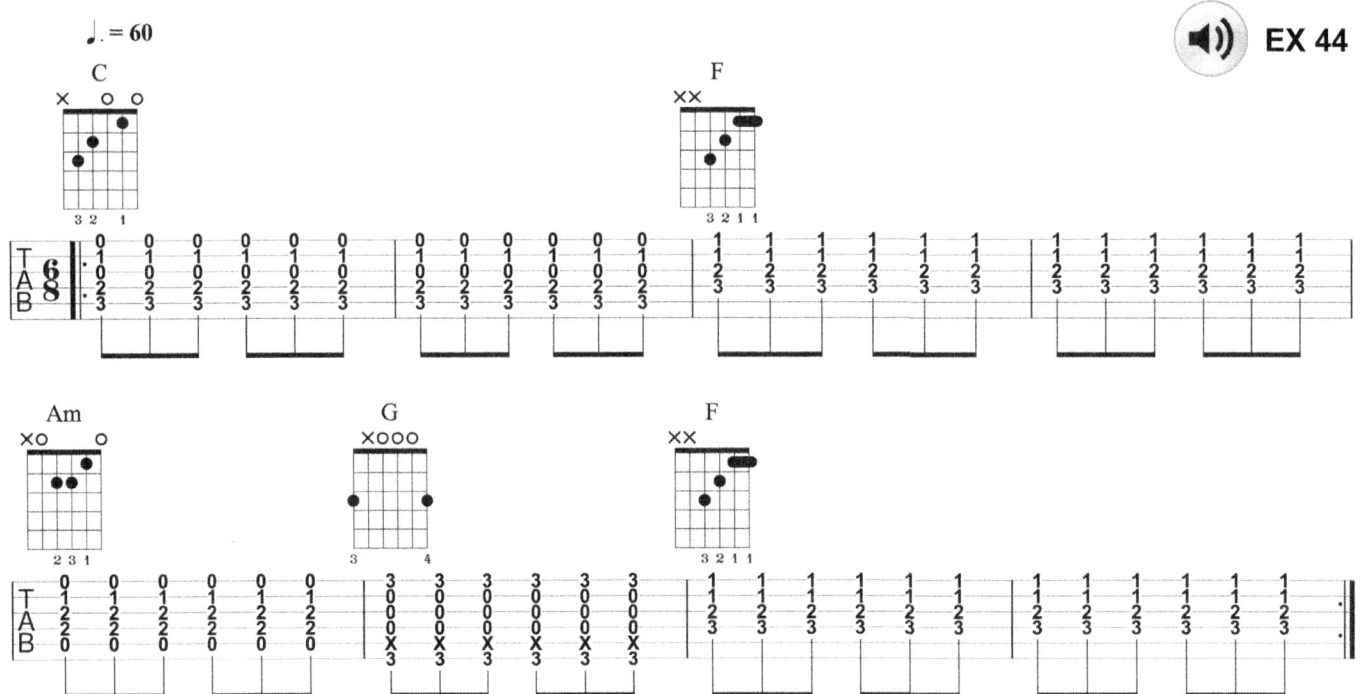

Now let's add some ornamentation to each chord. Although the chord frames above the tab make it seem like the harmony is changing in every bar, the truth is, the harmony is exactly the same as in the previous example—C–F–Am–G–F (I–IV–vi–V–IV)—only the embellishments here briefly imply sus2 and sus4 chords, which are illustrated in the chord frames.

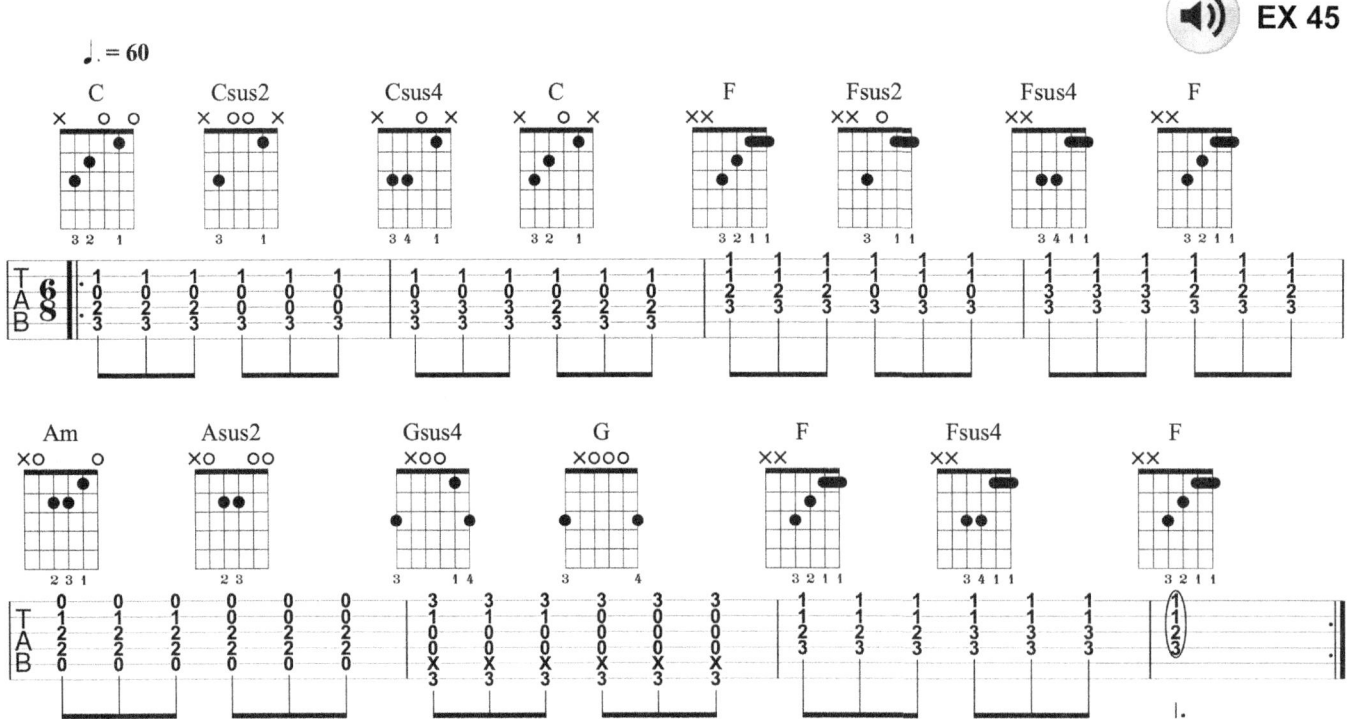

Notice how much more interesting the progression becomes by simply adding or subtracting a finger here and there. Plus, the ornamentation in this particular example creates a memorable—and singable—melody. Consequently, you get the best of both words—harmony *and* melody!

FULLY-FRETTED CHORD ORNAMENTATION

Now let's move up the fretboard a bit and apply ornamentation to some fully-fretted chords. First, let's take a look at the chords and progression that we'll be using:

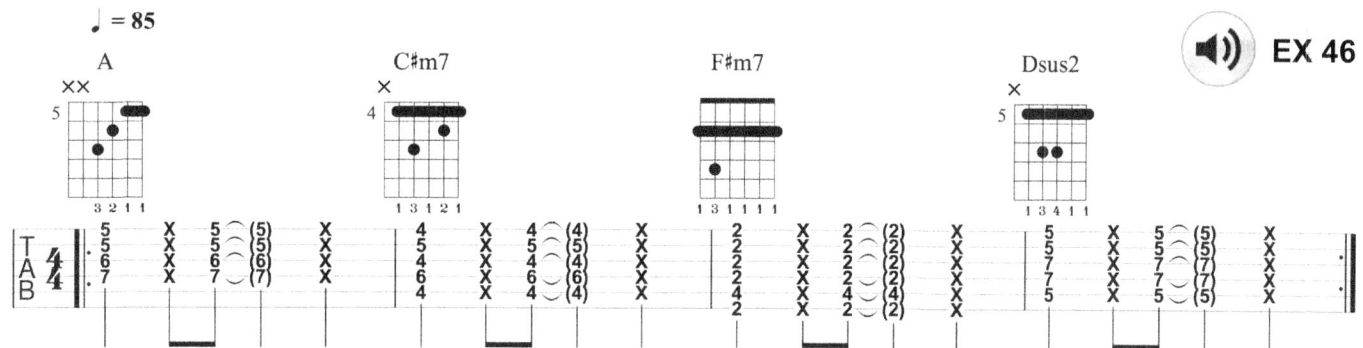

This progression, A–C#m7–F#m7–Dsus2 (I–iii–vi–IV in the key of A), features a major triad (A), two minor 7th chords (C#m7 and F#m7), and a suspended chord (Dsus2). Despite the differences in chord quality, all of these chords are prime for embellishment. For example, here's one way we can ornament these chords:

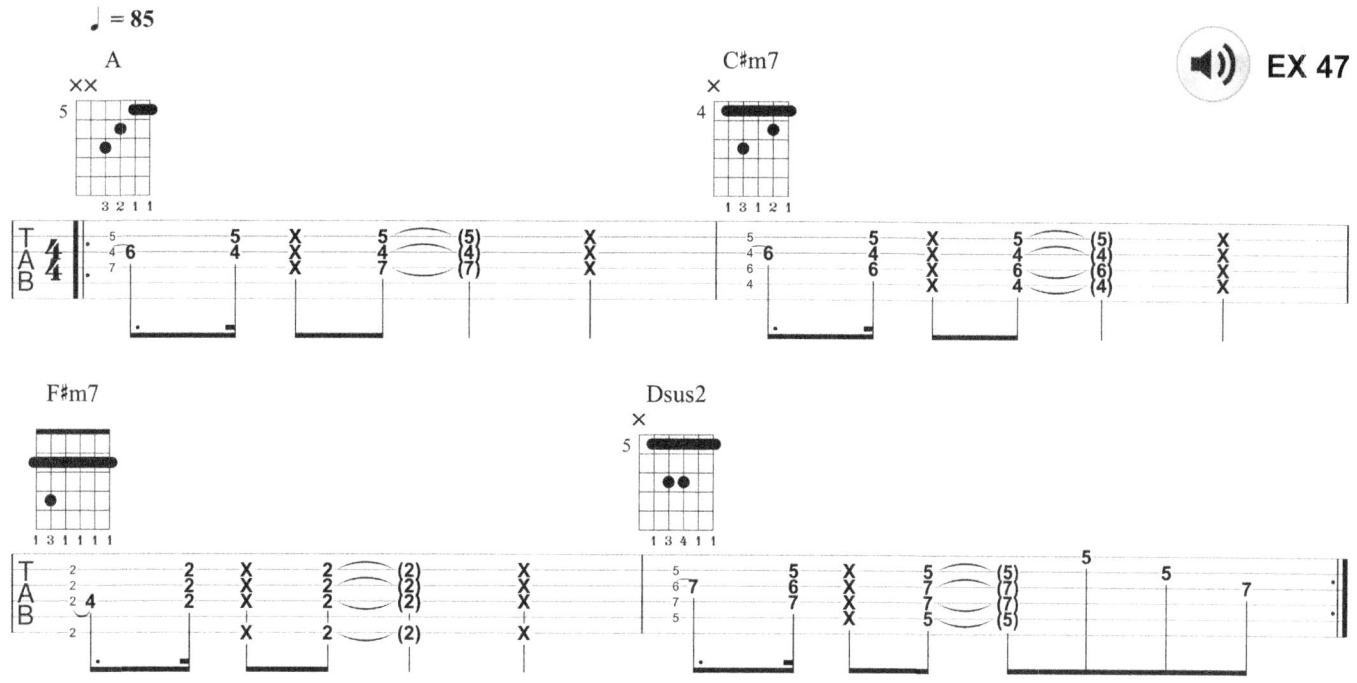

Quite a difference between the two examples, right? While there's a time and place for the first example (the strummed chords), the second example is something you could write a whole song around—it could serve as an intro, verse, *and* chorus and still retain interest.

Hammer-ons, pull-offs, and suspended (sus) chords are not the only way to embellish chords; another popular technique for chord embellishment is to incorporate double stops, particularly in conjunction with slides.

31

Let's take the progression that we've just been working on, A–C#m7–F#m7–Dsus2, and apply some double-stop embellishment, like this:

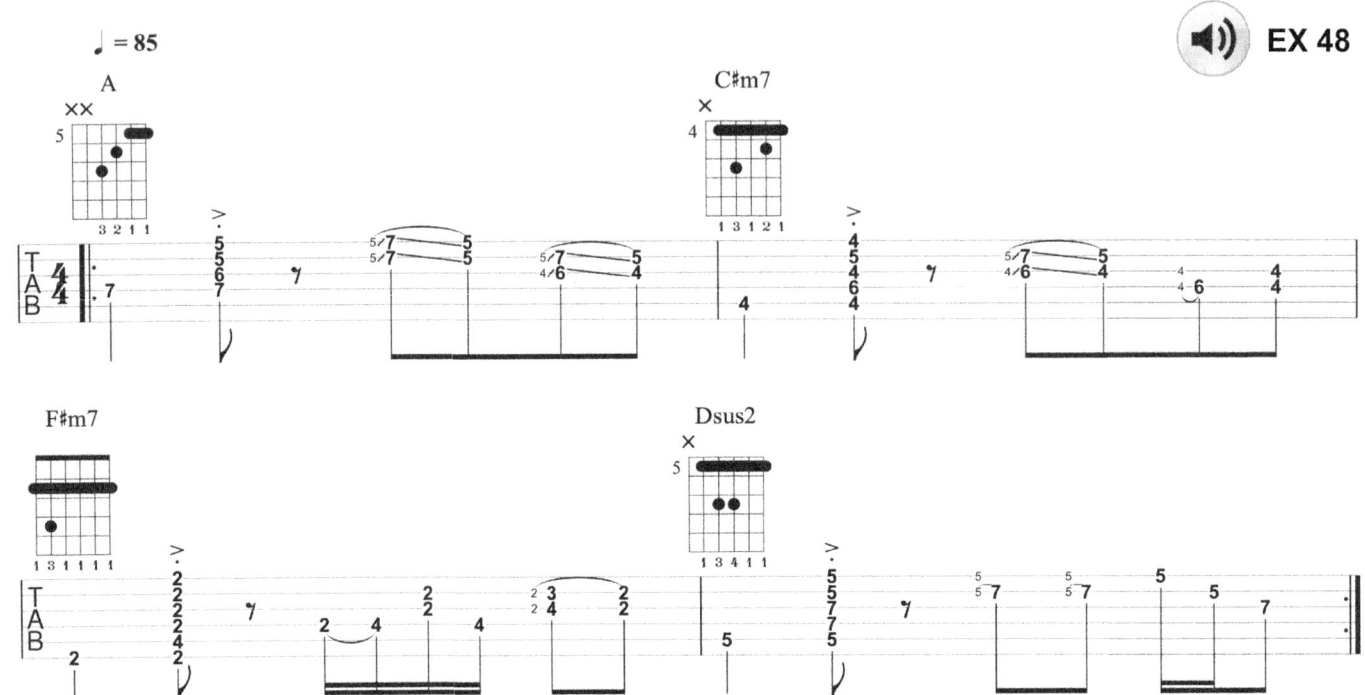

If you're a beginner—or even an intermediate guitarist—this type of riff may be a little too challenging right now, but the point of this example is to demonstrate that chords don't need to be static. On the contrary, you can take basic shapes like the ones in this example and incorporate notes from the surrounding fretboard area—and from the same key—and create interesting, melodic guitar riffs to use in your songs and compositions.

CHAPTER 7: OPEN-STRING DRONES

One of the most compelling characteristics of the guitar is the sound of ringing open strings, whether as part of an arpeggio pattern, a guitar riff, or a chord progression. We've touched on some of these applications in previous chapters, and now we're going to go over one of the most sonically powerful ways to utilize open strings—drones.

In music, a *drone* is a pitch—or *pitches*—that rings uninterrupted, usually while other notes or chords change around it. On guitar, drones can be bass strings, treble strings, or a combination of the two. In this chapter, we're going discuss both examples and how you can turn drones into instrumental guitar hooks that can define your song.

BASS-STRING DRONES

Nothing is more sonically powerful on guitar than creating riffs around a droning low-E string. What's even better is the fact that the adjacent string, A, happens to be the root of the IV chord in the key of E. Therefore, any riff you create with the droning low-E string can be reproduced a string higher, thereby implying a I–IV (E–A) chord change, like this:

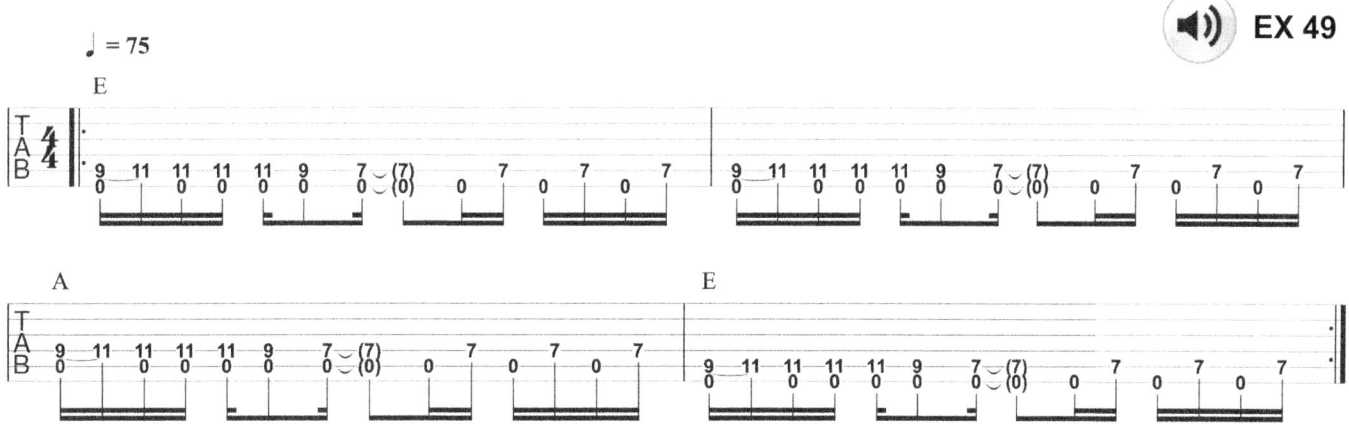

Notice the melodic interest that's created on the fretted strings while the low-E and A strings ring out to imply the E and A chord changes, respectively. Notice, too, how the octave roots (open strings and fretted pitches at fret 7) punctate each measure to really drive home the harmonies.

Now let's try a similar drone riff, this time starting on the open A string:

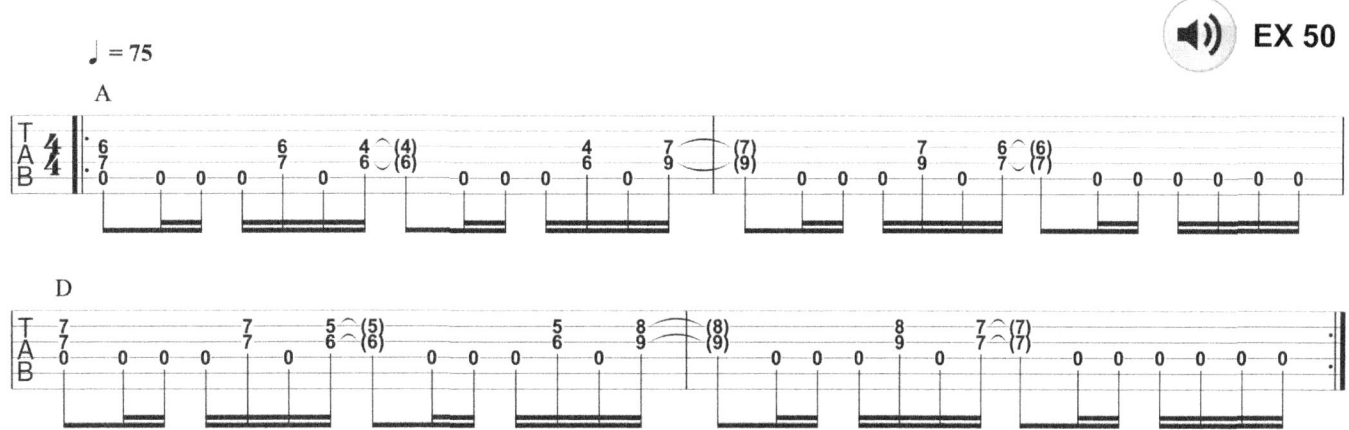

This riff juxtaposes an A-string drone and double stops played along strings 3–4. Again, notice how a melody is created on the fretted strings while the open string implies the harmony—in this case, A. Then, in bar 3, the idea is shifted up one string set to imply the IV chord, D. (Due to guitar's unique tuning, however, the double stops must be altered to accommodate the new chord, D.)

TREBLE-STRING DRONES

As mentioned in this chapter's introduction, drones don't have to be relegated to the bass strings. On the contrary, many cool ideas can be created by droning treble strings while shifting bass notes below them. Let's take a look at a few ideas.

This first example features a G-string drone that rings throughout the riff's four bars while the bass strings descend in stepwise fashion to imply a C–G/B–Am7–G progression.

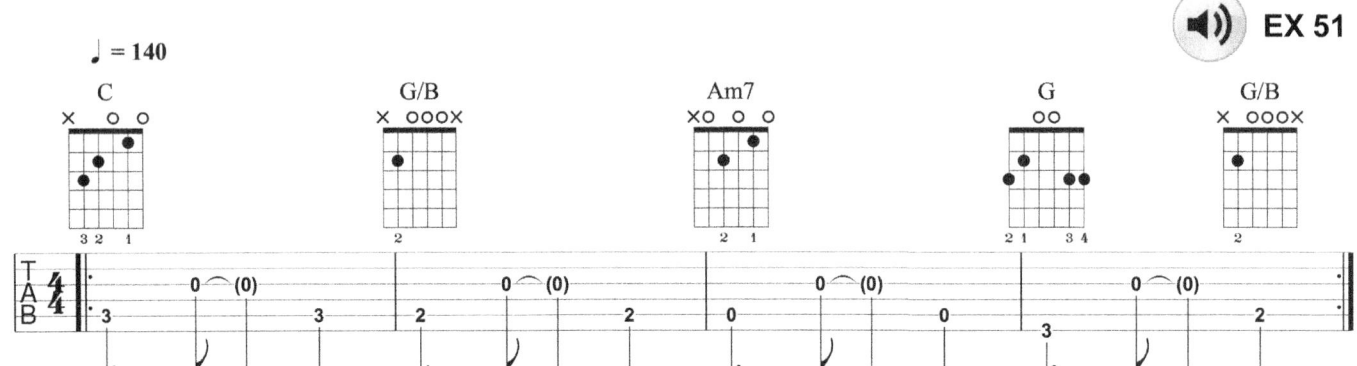

A whole song could be written around this drone idea by simply shifting the bass notes around. For example, we could start the song with our first riff, use it for the verse, and then rearrange the bass notes for a pre-chorus or chorus progression, like this:

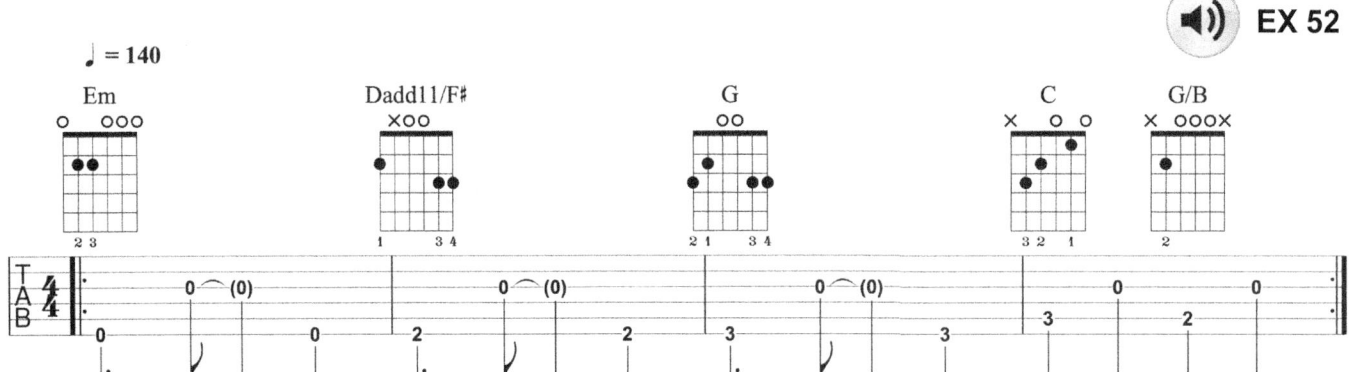

Now our bass notes ascend—rather than descend—in pitch, creating a nice contrast to our first riff. Our new progression, Em–Dadd11/F♯–G–C–G/B, also adds harmonic interest and keeps the music from becoming monotonous, which can become an issue when you've got an open string droning like the G string in these two examples.

Now let's try another string. Our next exercise features 10th-interval double stops played along the A and B strings, which are alternated with plucks of the open high-E string. While the 10ths imply a simple Em–D–G–C progression (i–VII–III–VI in E minor), the open high-E string adds harmonic color, giving us the set of changes listed above the staff: Em–Dadd9–G6–C.

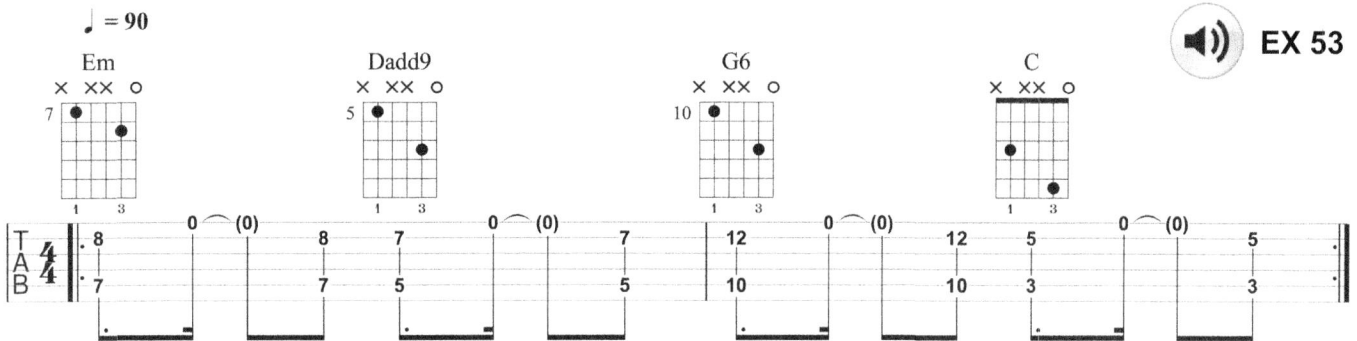

MULTI-STRING DRONES

Drones don't have to be relegate to one string, either. In fact, some cool multi-string drones can be created in the same fashion as our previous riffs. In the example below, bass notes descend the D string in stepwise fashion—A–G♯–F♯–E—while the open E and B strings ring uninterrupted. The result is an underlying A–G♯m–F♯m–E progression—a IV–iii–ii–I in the key of E.

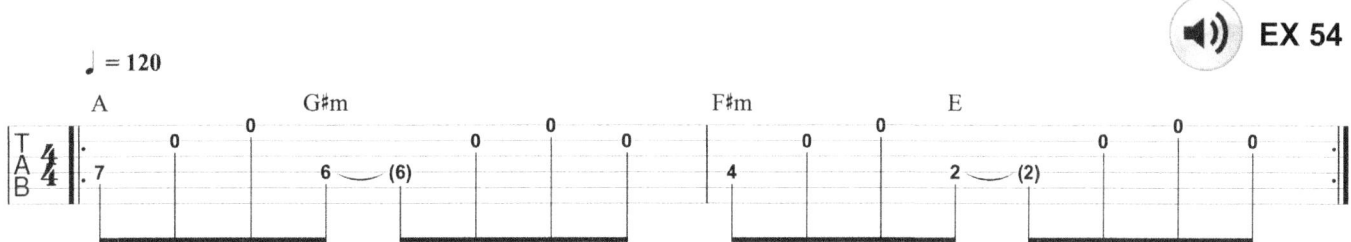

Now let's drone two non-adjacent open strings. The example below features the open high-E and D strings droning throughout the riff while two-note chord shapes are voiced on the B and G strings. The result is a loosely implied I–V–ii–I (D–A–Em–D) progression in the key of D (the "slash" chords, A/D and Em7/D, just mean that D is the lowest note of the chord—it's played "in the bass").

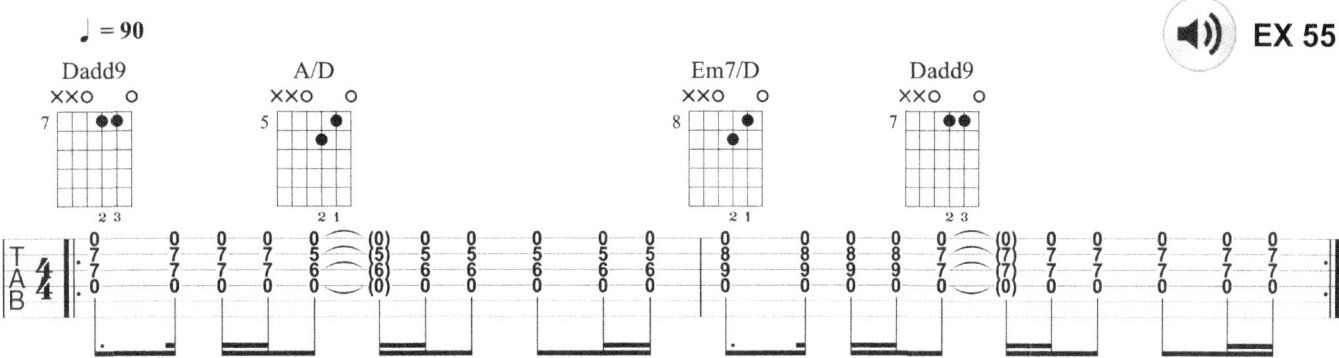

We can also pluck pairs of open strings in unison to create drone-based riffs:

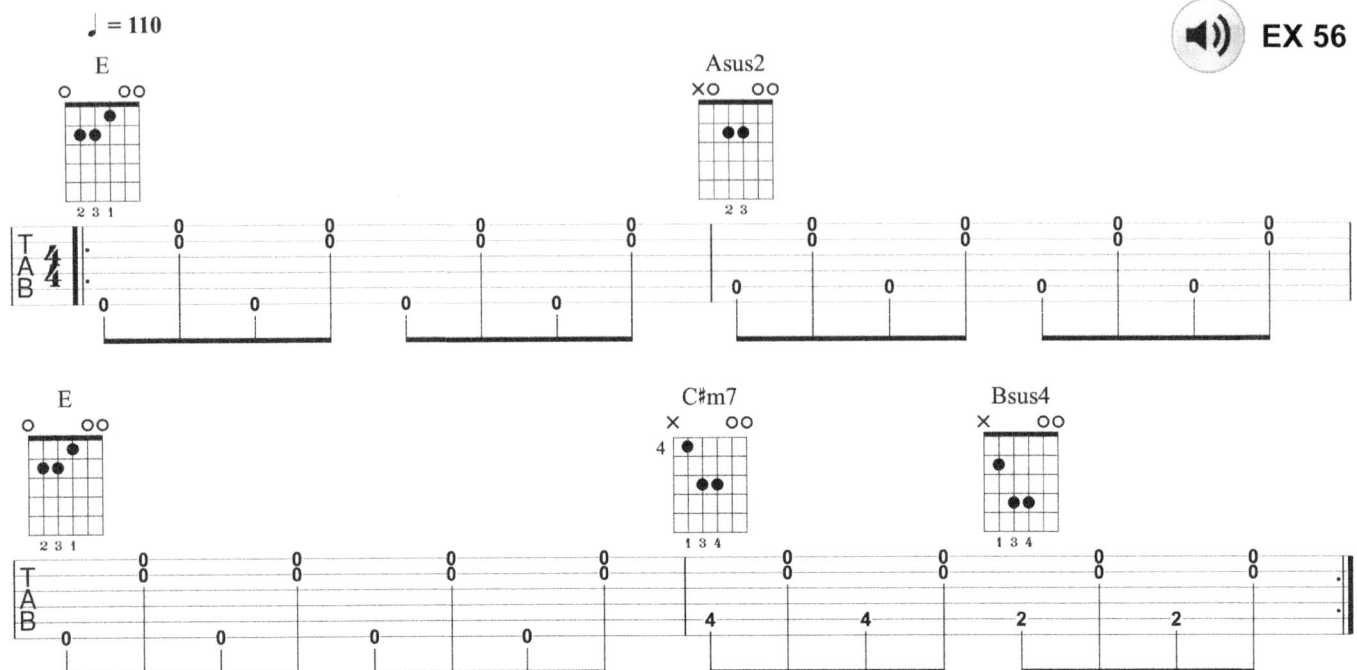

As the open high-E and B strings ring out, the bass notes shift between E, A, C♯, and B, implying an E–Asus2–E–C♯m7–Bsus4 progression (I–IV–I–vi–V in E major). The *full* chords, which are illustrated in the diagrams above the staff, can be strummed, as well, to create a fuller-sounding, more powerful drone riff. You'll hear this approach a lot in pop and rock music.

CHAPTER 8: OCTAVES AND DOUBLE STOPS

Octaves and double stops are also great tools for developing creative, guitar-centric song ideas. A *double stop*, which we touched on in the previous chapter, is simply two notes played simultaneously, typically (but not always) on adjacent strings. An *octave* also involves two notes being played simultaneously, but in this case, the two notes have the same pitch, just an octave (12 semitones) apart.

OCTAVES

On guitar, octaves can be used much like the drone examples from the previous chapter to create interesting guitar riffs. For example, in the figure below, the low-E string is droned while octaves are used to create a melody on top:

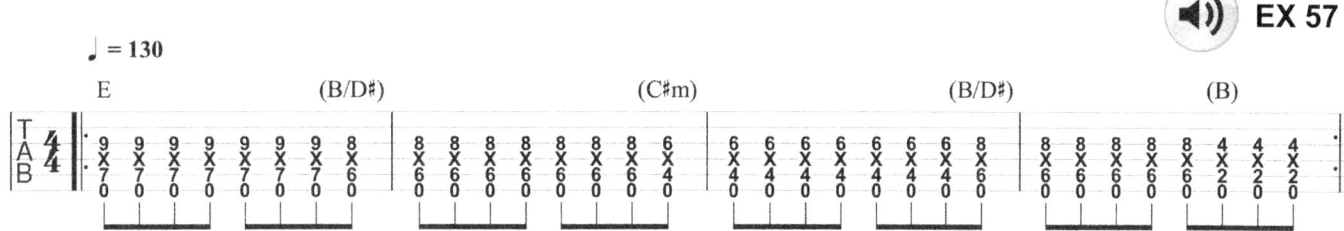

Sounds good, right? What's great about these types of riffs is that, harmonically, you could have the bass player either "pedal" the tonic note, E, throughout the riff or have him/her follow the changes implied by the octaves (indicated in parentheses above the staff). The E pedal will sound more powerful, whereas following the changes will create more harmonic interest.

Let's try another one, this time with an A-string drone:

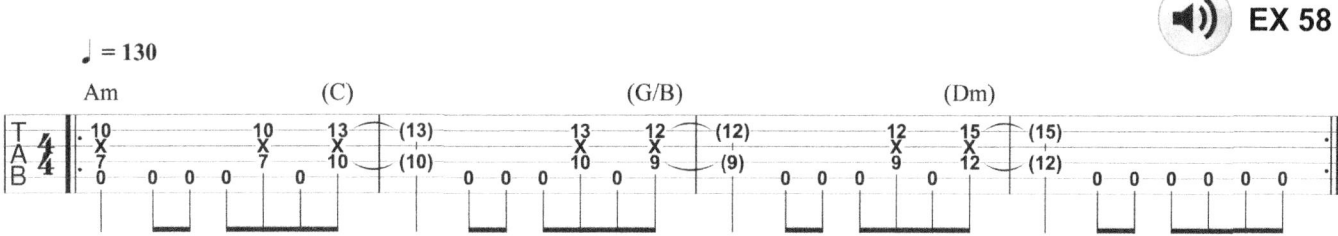

This one is a bit different in that it's in a minor key, Am, and the octaves and pedal tones are not always played at the same time. Like the previous example, however, the bass player can choose to either pedal an A note throughout or follow the changes implied by the octaves (indicated in parentheses).

As you can see, octaves are great tools for writing drone-based riffs. But that's not the only way to utilize them. Let's take a look at a couple of other ways we can use octaves to create guitar riffs. In the example below, power chords and octaves are combined to imply an A minor progression: Am–C–G–F–Em (i–III–VII–VI–v). Like the drone-based riffs, the octaves infuse this example with some ear-catching melody, creating a riff that is far more interesting than one played exclusively with power chords.

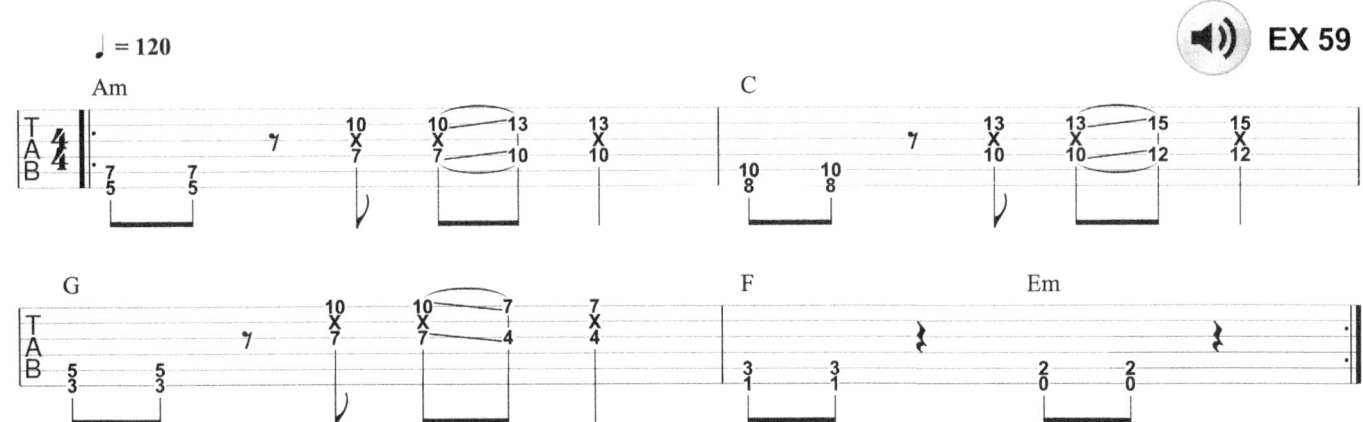

EX 59

Let's try one more. This next riff is entirely comprised of octaves played along the low-E and D strings. By moving them up and down the fretboard, the octaves imply a non-diatonic G major progression: G–F–G–Bb–C (I–bVII–I–bIII–IV). Notice how a simple concept like adding a couple of well-placed eighth-note rests (on the downbeat of bars 2 and 4) gives the riff a touch of syncopation—and a whole lot of character!

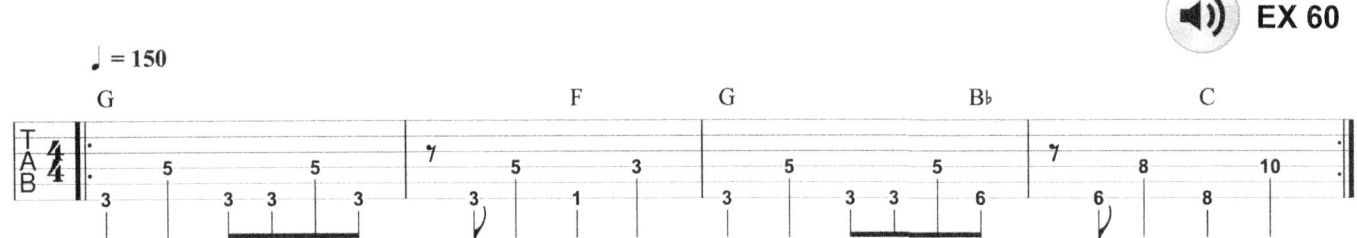

EX 60

DOUBLE STOPS
Now let's switch our attention to double stops. Although we've covered double stops previously, in this section, we're going to delve a little deeper into how we can use them to write creative guitar riffs for songs and compositions.

Major and Minor 3rds
Major and minor 3rds are two of the most common double stops used by guitarists. These shapes are illustrated on the high-E and B strings in the figures below:

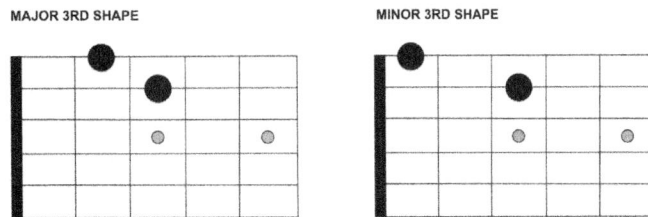

These shapes can be applied to any pair of adjacent strings, except for B and G, which are voiced with the shapes below:

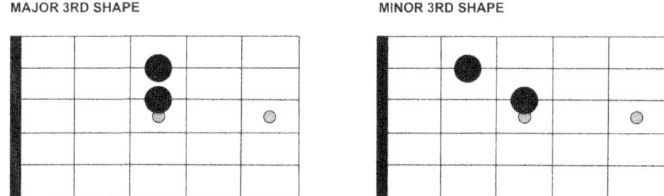

Let's apply these shapes to the A and D strings and use the low-E string as a pedal, or drone. The following riff is a little funky and tricky to perform, so be sure to listen to the audio track to hear how it sounds. By moving the major and minor 3rd shapes up and down the neck, we imply an E–F#m–G#m–F#m progression (I–ii–iii–ii in the key of E major).

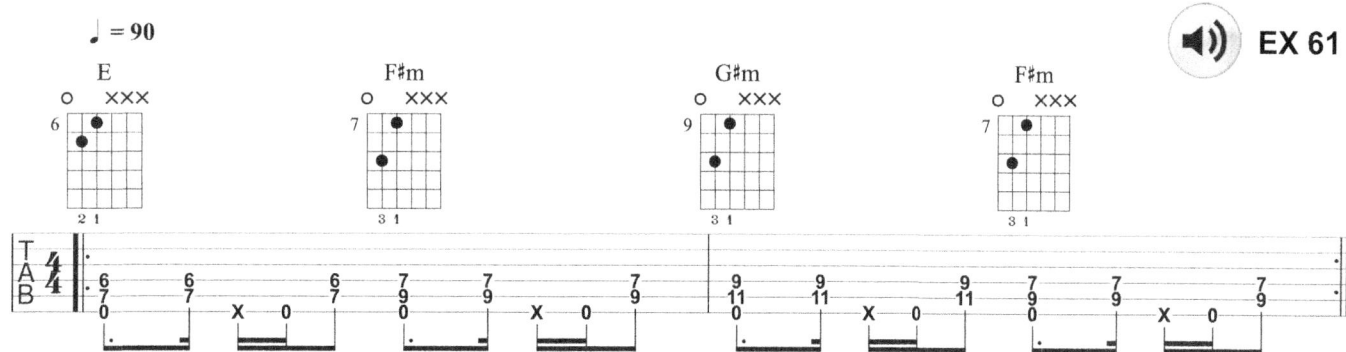

Now let's apply this same idea to the B and G strings, which will require some finger adjustments due to the new shapes. Instead of E major, let's transpose the idea to D major and use the open D string as the pedal:

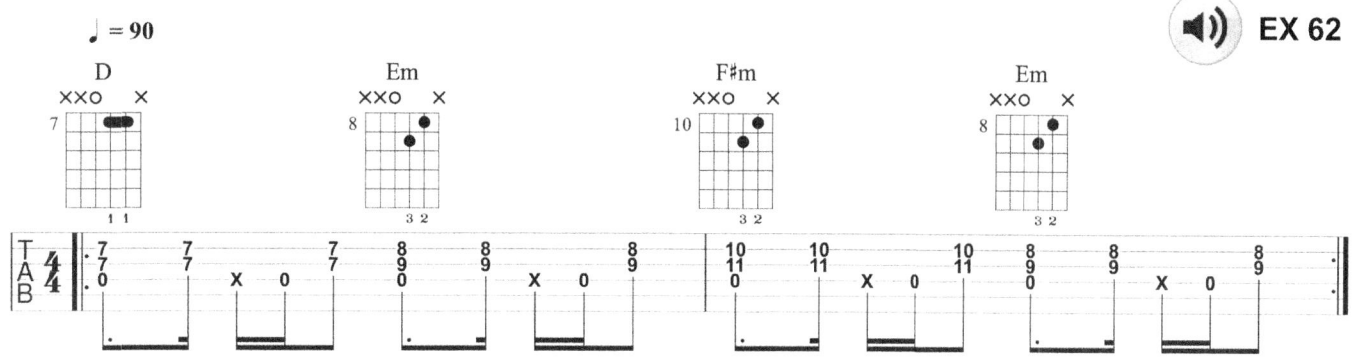

Double stops are simply two-note chords, and like any chord, we can arpeggiate the notes instead of plucking or strumming them. Let's take the I–ii–iii–ii progression that we used in the previous two examples, transpose it to the key of G, apply it to the high-E and B strings, and arpeggiated the major and minor 3rd shapes instead of plucking them, like this:

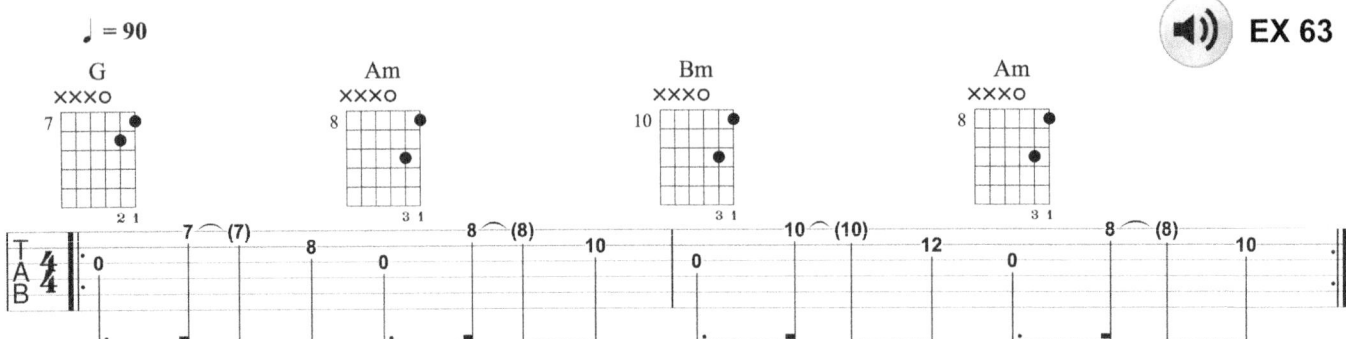

Major and Minor 6ths

Another pair of popular double stops among guitar players are the major and minor 6th shapes. Here are the shapes that are used when 6ths are applied to either the low-E and D strings or the A and G strings:

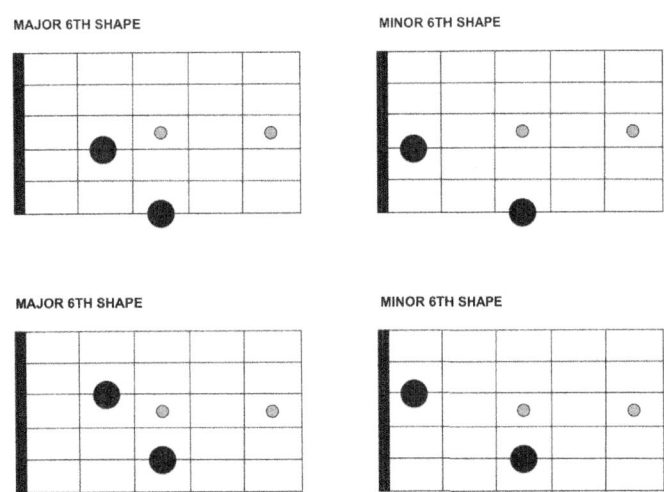

Like the major and minor 3rds, 6ths have two sets of shapes, depending on which strings they're played on. Here are the major and minor 6th shapes when applied to either the D and B strings or the G and high-E strings:

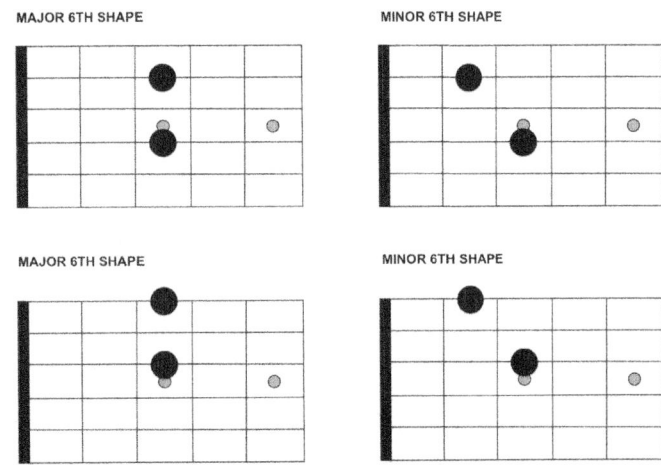

Let's take a look at a couple of ways we can utilize these 6ths to create some stellar guitar parts. Our first riff features the major and minor 6th shapes voiced along the A and G strings while the low E string is pedaled in the bass. There's no real harmonic movement in this riff; instead, the 6ths imply different "colors" of E major, particularly E6 and E7.

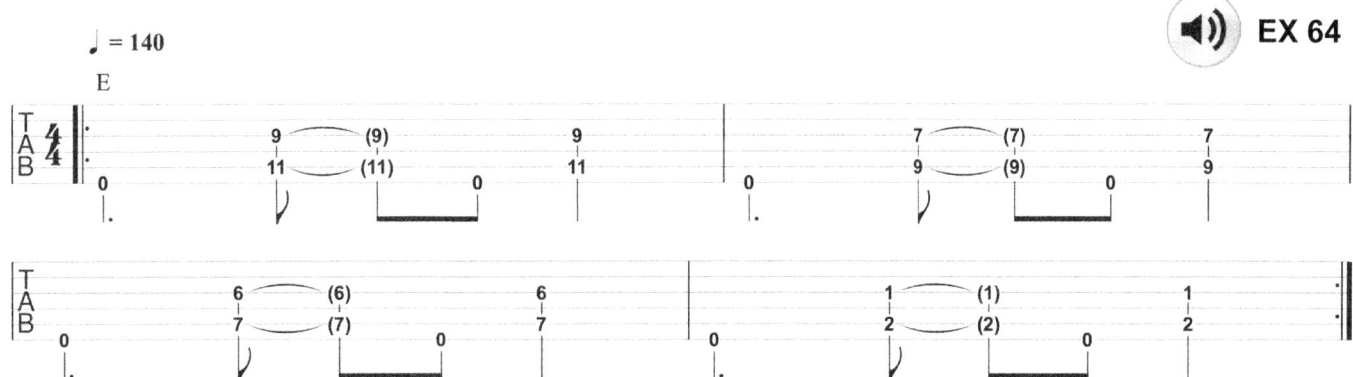

EX 64

Now let's shift this idea to the D and B strings, which will require the alternate voicings of the major and minor 6th shapes. Instead of playing the riff in its original key, E major, let's transpose it to A major and use the open A string as a pedal, like this:

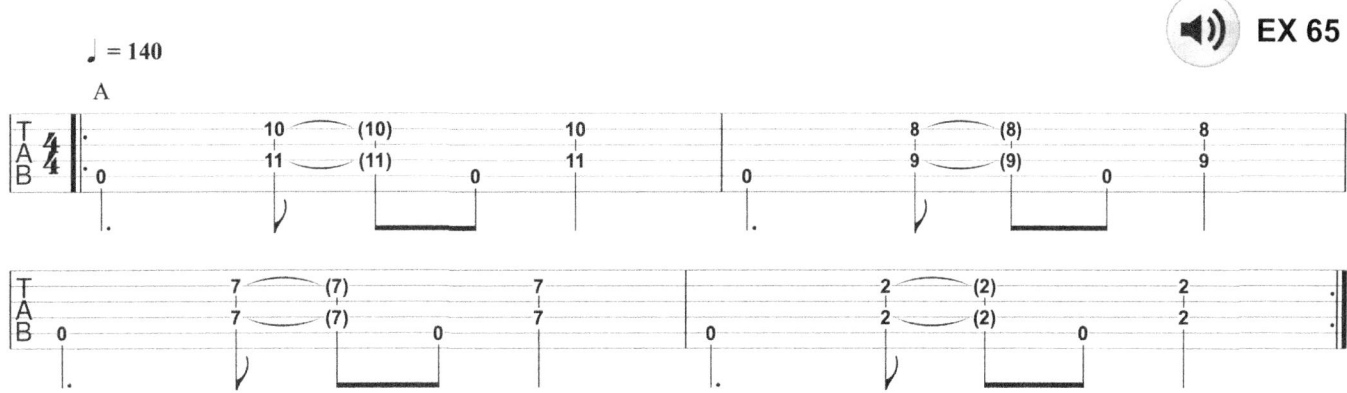

EX 65

This type of riff can be heard in Eric Clapton's "Change the World" and shines brightest as the focal point (i.e., instrument hook) of the song, whether in pop, folk, rock, or country. Additionally, these shapes are versatile enough to work in a vast array of tempos, including ballads, mid-tempo songs, and even uptempo grooves.

Just because these major and minor 6ths are voiced on non-adjacent strings doesn't mean we can't arpeggiate them. On the contrary, arpeggiating these shapes is a great way to spark an idea. Here's an example to get you started:

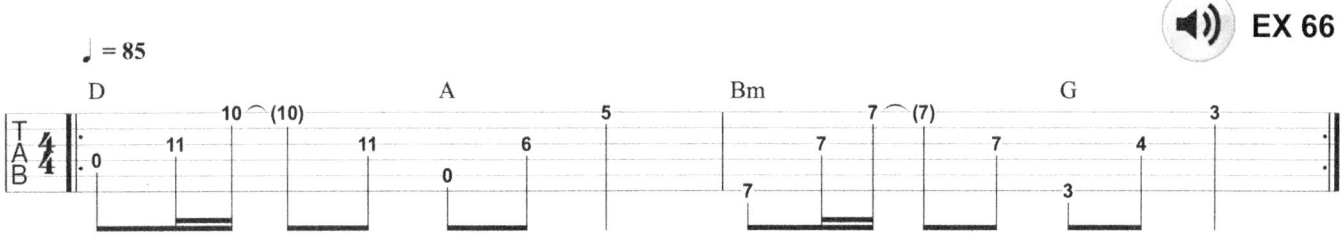

EX 66

While the open D string could have been pedaled underneath the 6ths throughout, I decided to change the bass notes to reflect the chord changes in order to more strongly imply the D–A–Bm–G chord progression (I–V–vi–IV in D major). Once you're able to play the example as written, try playing the version below, which features the D-string pedal.

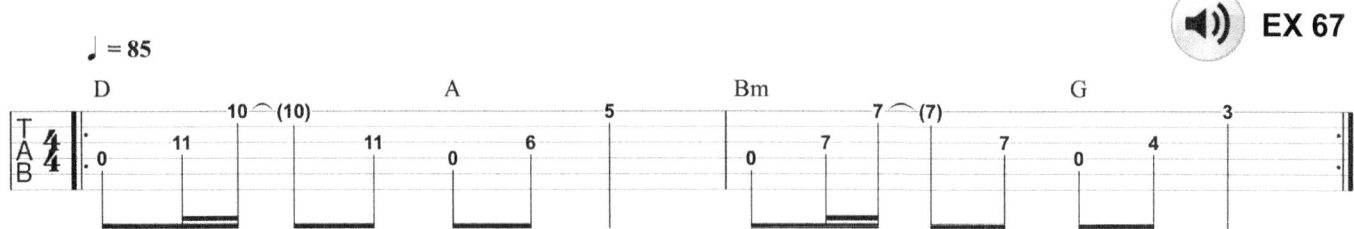

Each has its own vibe, right? To me, the first one feels a bit uninspired, whereas the second one—the one with the D-string pedal—is slightly darker and more emotive. Nevertheless, both versions are viable songwriting options—it just depends on what vibe you're going for.

CHAPTER 9: ARPEGGIOS

One of the easiest ways for a guitarist to get creative on his/her instrument is to experiment with arpeggiating the chords of common progressions. Instead of strumming the chords, which can come across as rather dull, the notes are plucked individually. And the great thing about arpeggios is that you can pluck the notes of each chord in several different ways, which gives you countless note combinations. Let's take a look at a few...

CHORD-BASED ARPEGGIOS

Let's start with a basic I–vi–V–IV progression in the key of C: C–Am–G–F. Here's how the chords sound if we strum them in a straightforward manner:

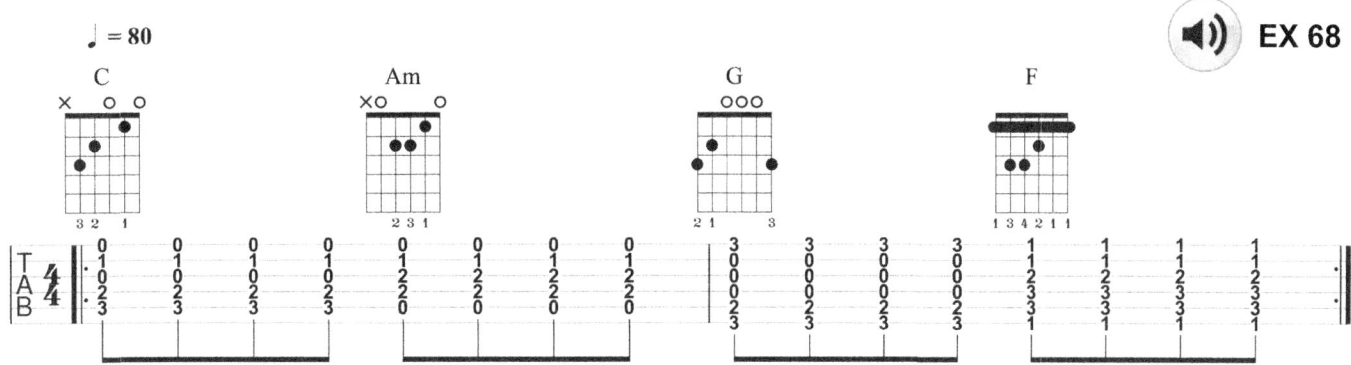

Now let's take our C, Am, G, and F chords and arpeggiate each one, moving from the lowest note in the chord to the highest while using the rhythm from our previous example.

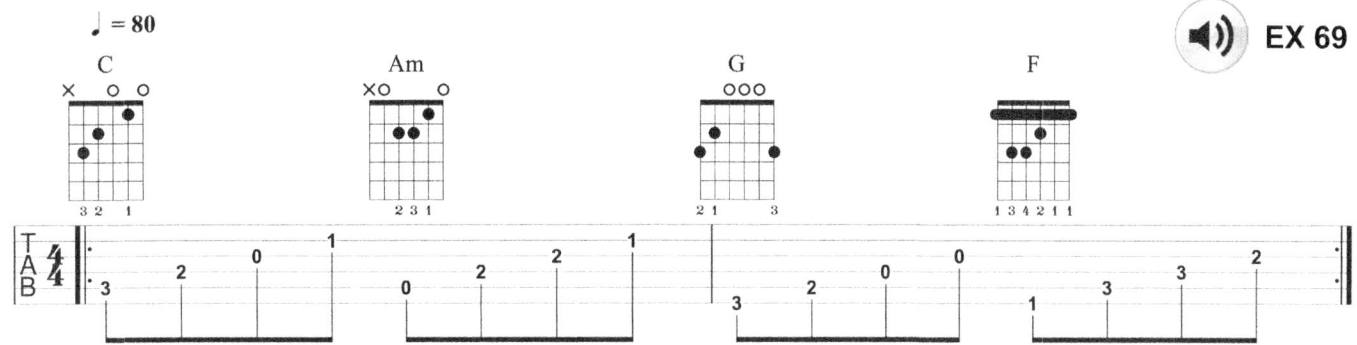

Sounds pretty good, right? While strumming certainly has its place, arpeggios can sometimes be the missing ingredient in your songs.

Now let's switch things up a bit and *descend* the arpeggios. We'll start by picking the root note on the downbeat of each chord change and then descend the treble strings, like this:

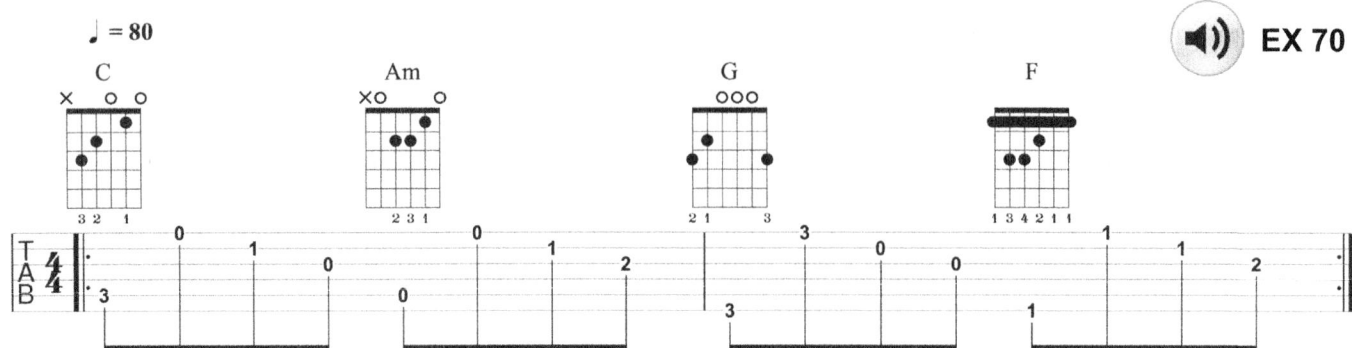

Arpeggios don't have to continuously move from high to low or low to high; on the contrary, some great patterns can be created by alternating between bass and treble strings. The example below demonstrates this approach.

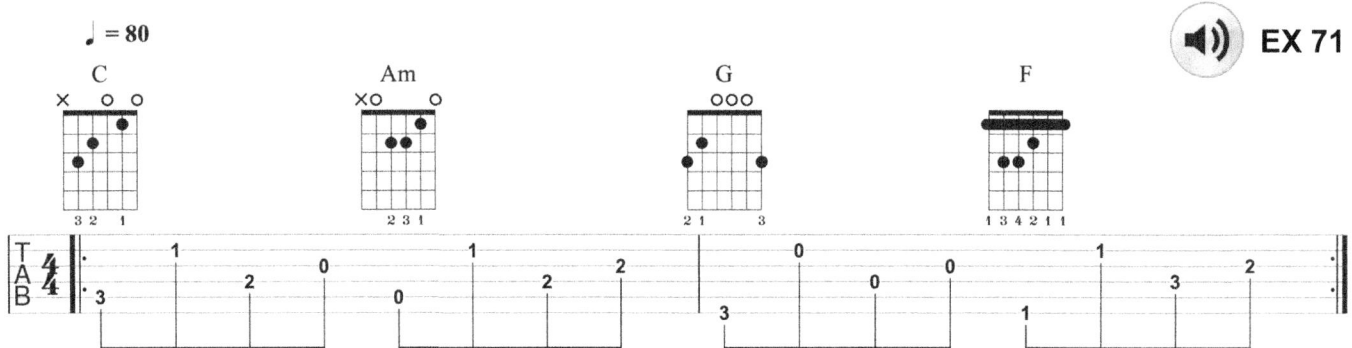

Notice that, although the bass notes move from string 5 (measure 1) to string 6 (measure 2), the rest of the picking for each chord alternates between strings 2, 4, and 3, respectively. This results in a repetitive yet evolving melodic passage—a counter melody to whatever melody you might play or sing on top of it.

Open-chord arpeggios also work really well in other time signatures, particularly 6/8. In the example below, the C, Am, G, and F chords from the previous examples are ascended and descend over the course of one measure each. This type of riff is similar to the one played in the Animals' "House of the Rising Sun."

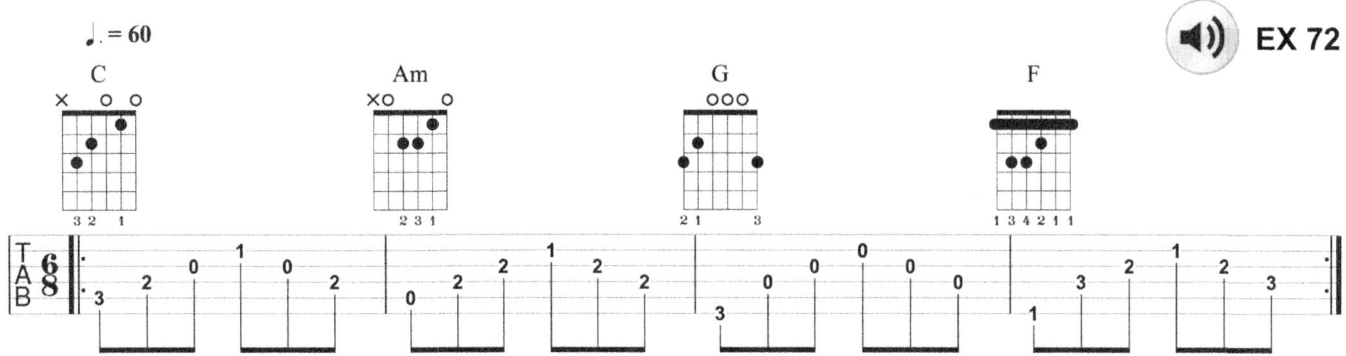

SINGLE-NOTE ARPEGGIOS

Arpeggios don't have to be chord-based, either. In fact, some of the greatest rock riffs of all time are based on single-note arpeggios like the one below.

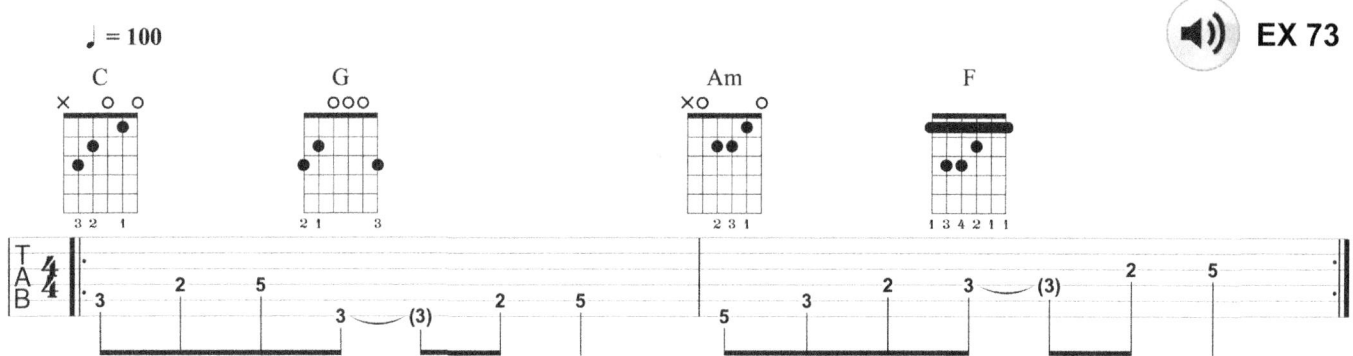

In this riff, single notes are played on the bass strings to outline a C–G–Am–F progression (the same four chords we've been playing throughout this chapter, only in a different order). The main difference between this type of riff and the chord-based ones is that the notes are not allowed to ring out, which is partly due to back-to-back notes being voiced on the same string.

Let's try one more before wrapping up this chapter. This next example is something you might hear Dave Matthews or the Police's Andy Summers play. The riff features single-note lines comprised of arpeggiated sus2 (suspended 2nd) chords. Despite the "sus2" labels, the chord changes are simply a variation on the C–Am–G–F progression from early, only now we're implying an Am–C–G–F progression.

The left-hand stretches are challenging, so take this one slowly at first. Rhythmically, this riff shouldn't give you too much trouble, however, because it's nearly identical to the rhythm of our previous example.

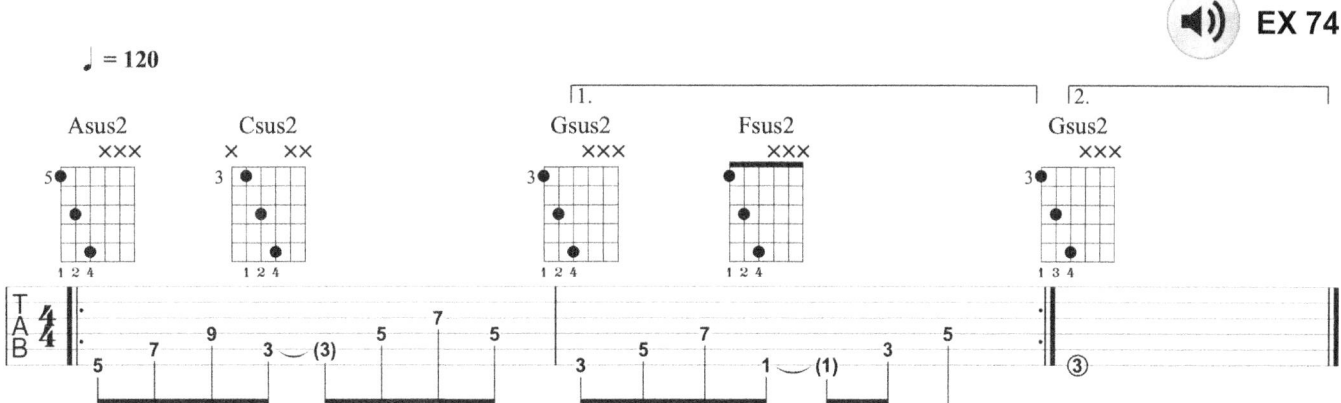

CHAPTER 10: 10TH INTERVALS

One of the most creative ways to transform your basic chord progression into something that is infinitely more ear-catching is to use wide-interval shapes like 10ths.

THE THEORY ON 10THS

A *10th interval* is simply a two-note chord that includes its root and 3rd (the first two notes of a triad); however, instead of playing the two notes in the same octave, the 3rd is displaced by an octave. For example, let's take a look at a common C major chord:

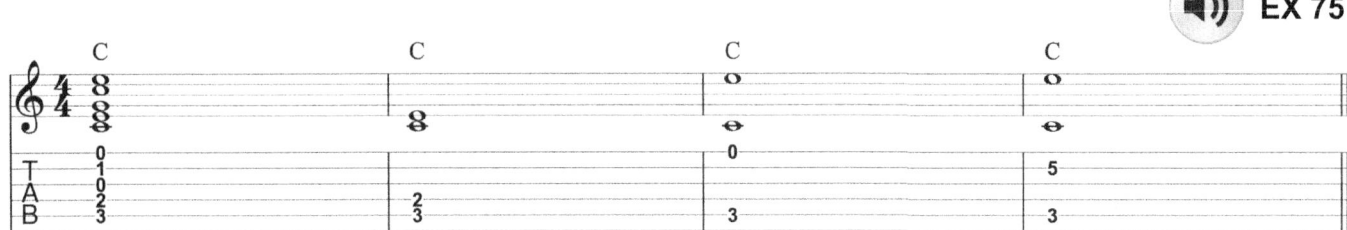

The first measure features a standard open C chord. The bottom (lower) three notes comprise the C triad—C–E–G (root–3rd–5th)—while the notes on strings 1–2 are the root (C) and 3rd (E) played in the higher octave. In other words, the same notes as on strings 5–4, just played one octave higher.

If we play the bottom two notes, C and E, together (measure 2), we are playing notes that are a 3rd (interval) apart. This is based on the major scale, where each note is given a number: **C**–D–**E**–F–G–A–B (**1**–2–**3**–4–5–6–7). If we count up from C to E, we arrive at 3, or the 3rd note of the major scale.

We can also continue counting beyond the octave C, like this: **C**–D–**E**–F–G–A–B–**C**–D–**E**–F–G–A–B (**1**–2–**3**–4–5–6–7–**8**–9–**10**–11–12–13). As you can see, the octave root is labeled "8," whereas the octave 3rd is labeled "10." In other words, the octave E is 10 scale steps higher than the original C root note. This interval, the 10th, is shown in measure 3. Another, more common way to play this interval is shown in measure 4.

The great thing about the voicing in measure 4 is that you can play its parallel minor, Cm, by simply lowering the B-string note by one fret:

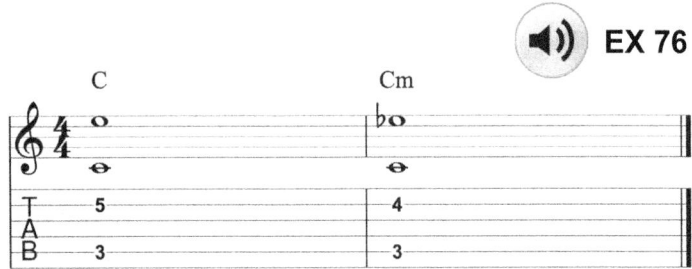

46

These shapes can also be applied to strings 6 and 3. Here's how our major and minor 10ths look on this string set, shown here in the key of G:

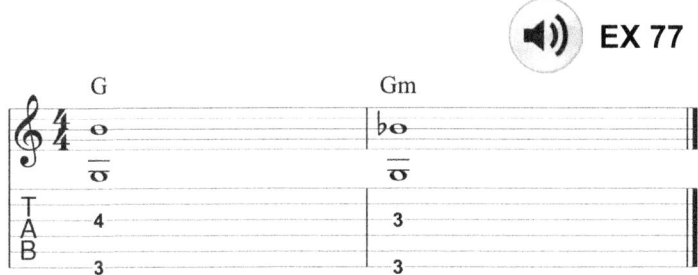

FIFTH-STRING SHAPES

Perhaps the most famous example of 10th intervals in pop music is the Beatles' classic "Blackbird." This interval shape also had a profound effect on guitar playing in the late '90s, when John Frusciante made a triumphant return to the Red Hot Chili Peppers and released the seminal "Scar Tissue." However, the popularity of 10ths hit its pinnacle in a five-year span from 2015 to 2020, when everyone from Justin Bieber ("Love Yourself") to Dan + Shay ("All to Myself") where crafting songs around this beloved interval.

Let's take a look at a couple of ways you can turn your standard chord progressions into ear-catching instrumental hooks. Let's start with a common i–III–VI–VII progression in E minor: Em–G–C–D:

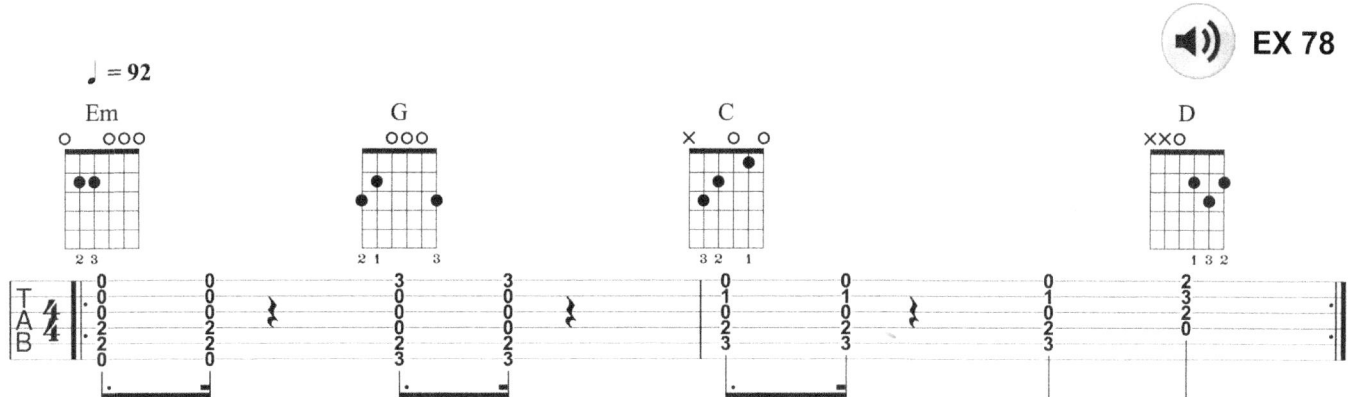

Not bad. But if we take those same chord changes and play them as 10ths along strings 5 and 2, we get a whole new vibe:

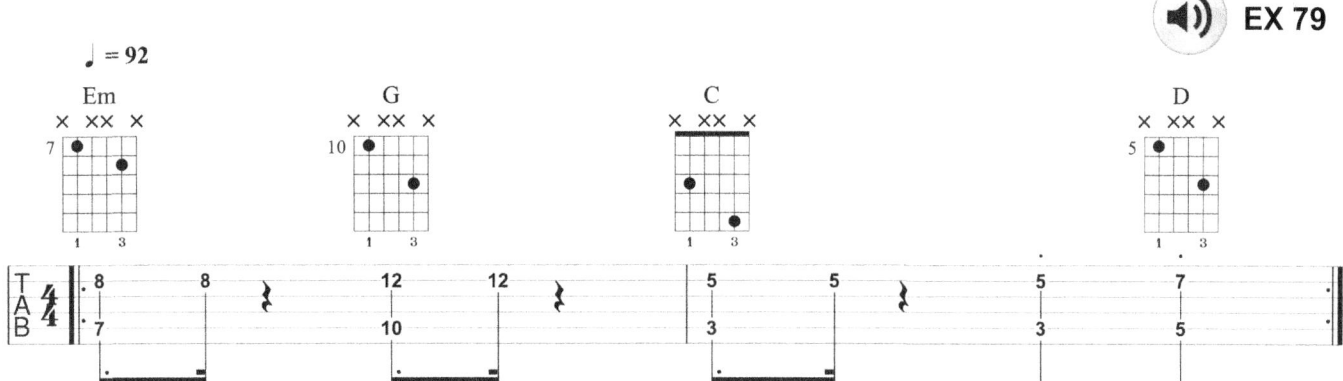

SIXTH-STRING SHAPES

Let's try another one, but this time applying the major and minor 10ths to strings 6 and 3. The progression we'll be using here is A–C#m–F#m–D (I–iii–vi–IV in A major):

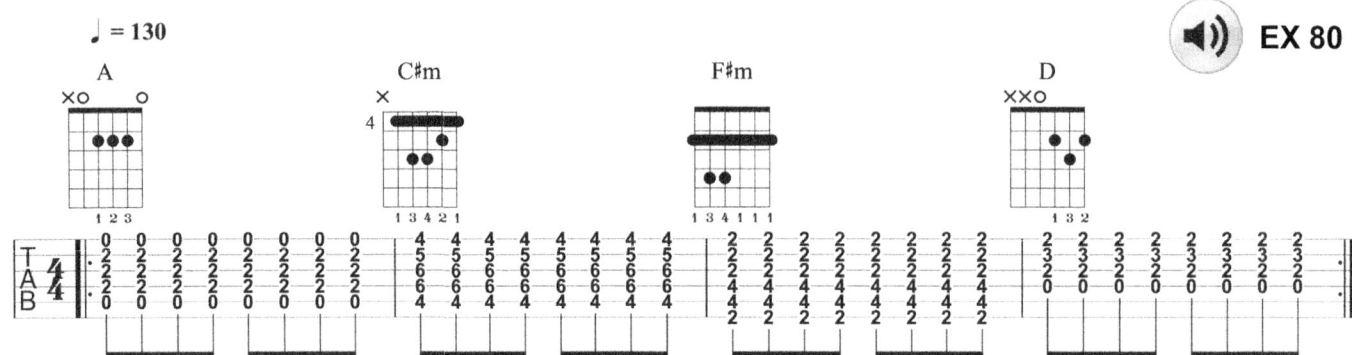

The iii chord, C#m, gives the progression some harmonic color, but let's see what happens when we play the exact same rhythm but replace the open chords and barre chords with 10th intervals:

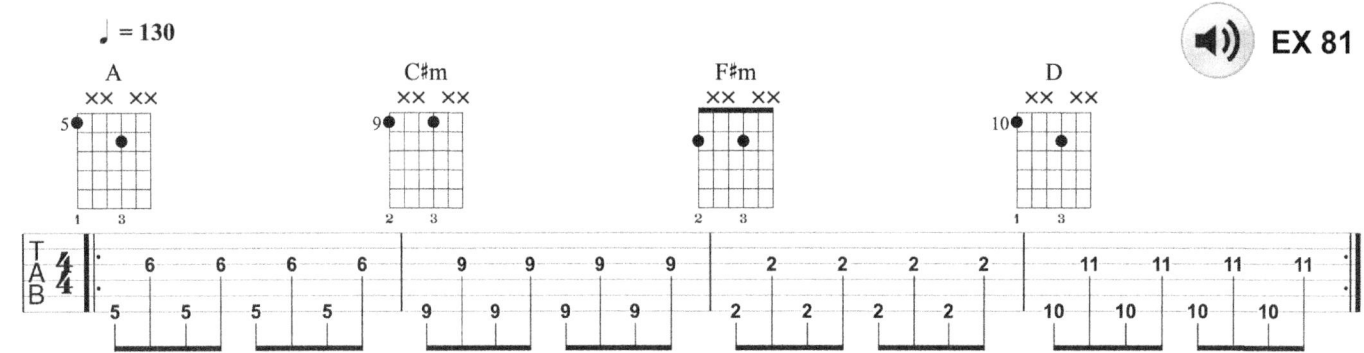

Better, right? Well, maybe not "better," but the 10ths certainly convey a different mood, or vibe.

COMBINING SHAPES

Let's finish this chapter with one more example. This time, we're going to juxtapose 5th- and 6th-string shapes to perform a i–III–VII–VI–VII progression in B minor: Bm–D–A–G–A. Let's start by playing the progression with common triad voicings:

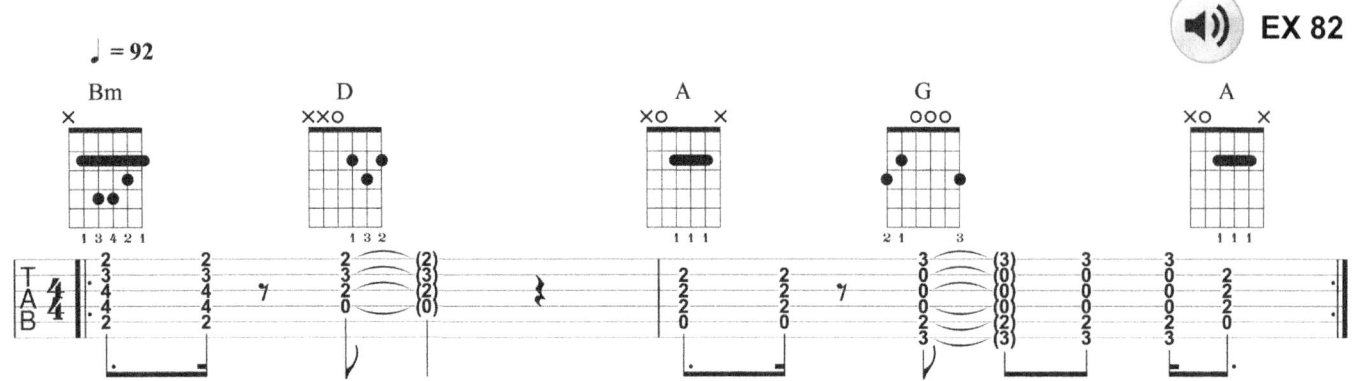

48

Now let's hear how the progression sounds with 10ths:

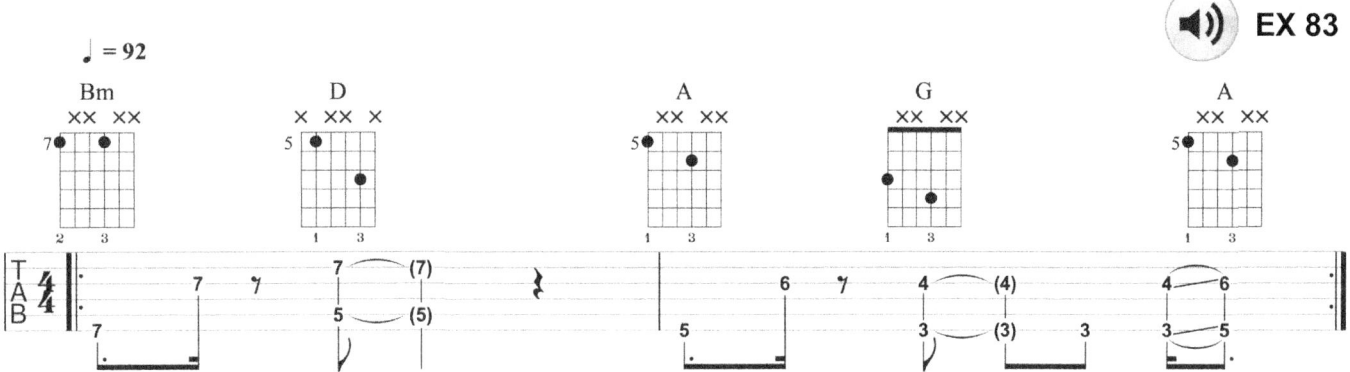

Pretty cool, right? While the strummed chords certainly set a mood, the 10ths give the progression an identity, one that catches the ear of the listener right away. We've all heard strummed chords a thousand times, but the 10ths are a (relatively) fresh sound!

The next step is to practice playing some of your favorite progressions with these 10th shapes. To do so, simply locate the root of each chord on either the 5th or 6th string and then adjust the shape to accommodate its major or minor quality.

CHAPTER 11: HARMONIC RHYTHM

As songwriters and composers, we often get so wrapped up in finding the "right" chords or melody that we sometimes forget to focus on the other part of the equation—rhythm. The term *harmonic rhythm* refers to the duration of each chord within a chord progression. Just as certain combination of notes and chords can convey certain emotions, rhythm can have an equally profound effect on your music. In this chapter, we'll look at several ways to take your chord progressions to the next level by simply experimenting with different harmonic rhythms.

BASIC HARMONIC RHYTHM

Let's start with a common IV–I–vi–V progression in G major: C–G–Em–D. To give it a little more character, we'll substitute Cadd9 for the C major triad, and Em7 for the Em triad. Here's this progression played in simple whole notes:

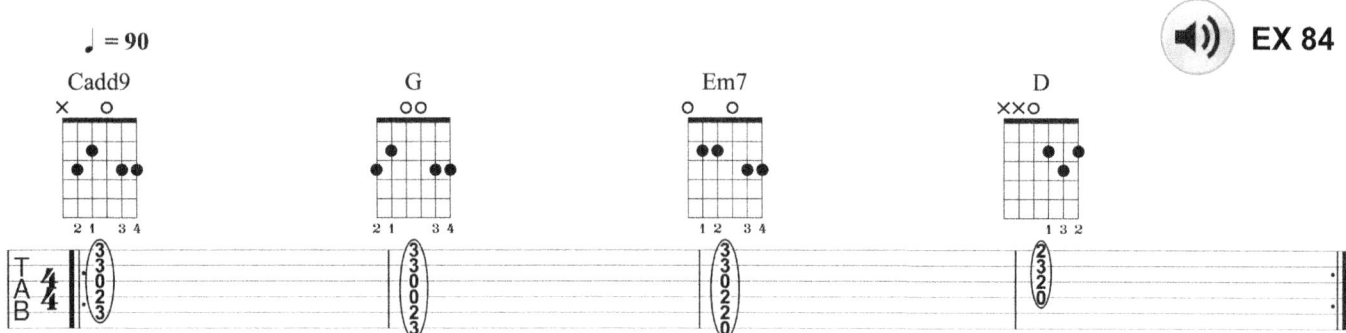

Rhythmically, this is about as basic as you can get. While whole notes work in certain situations—for example, in chordal "pads," slow ballads, or songs with fast tempos—they generally offer little rhythmic excitement.

Now let's play our same Cadd9–G–Em7–D progression, but this time, we'll change chords every two beats (i.e., in a half-note rhythm), like this:

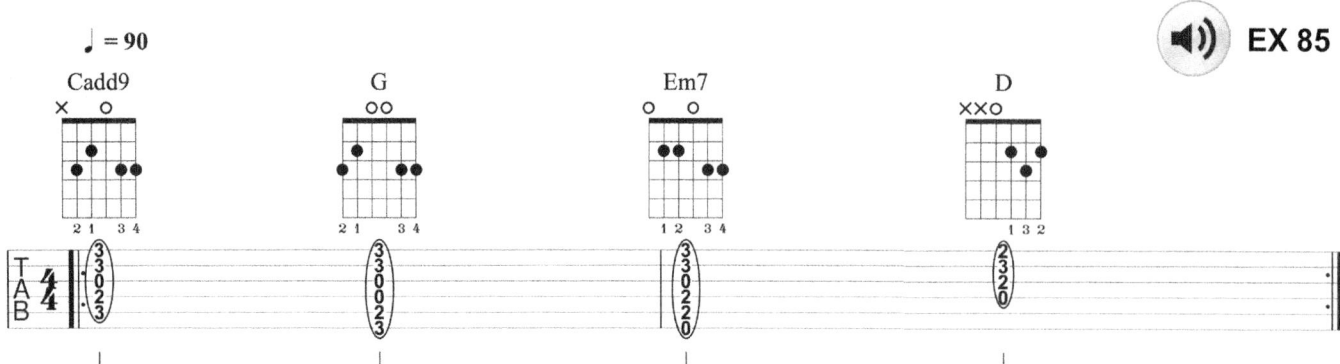

By simply speeding up the rate of the chord changes (i.e., playing two per measure instead of one), the energy of the progression is increased. This is magnified when you have a rhythm section (bass and drums) playing behind you—heck, even the click of a metronome will convey the increased energy.

When I'm producing music, one of the things I'm always checking is whether or not the music is "dragging." In other words, is there a rhythmic subdivision (quarter notes, eighth notes, 16ths, etc.) that is keeping the music energetic and moving forward? Nothing will turn off listeners like music that lacks energy.

SYNCOPATION

Another rhythmic trick you can use to increase the energy and excitement of your chord progressions is syncopation. The term *syncopation* refers to any rhythm that stresses weak beats, or off-beats; for example, eighth-note rhythms that stress the "and" portion of the beat. The degree of syncopation can vary from quite simple (disco hi-hats) to rather complex (funk bass lines).

Let's take our previous example and add some simple syncopation:

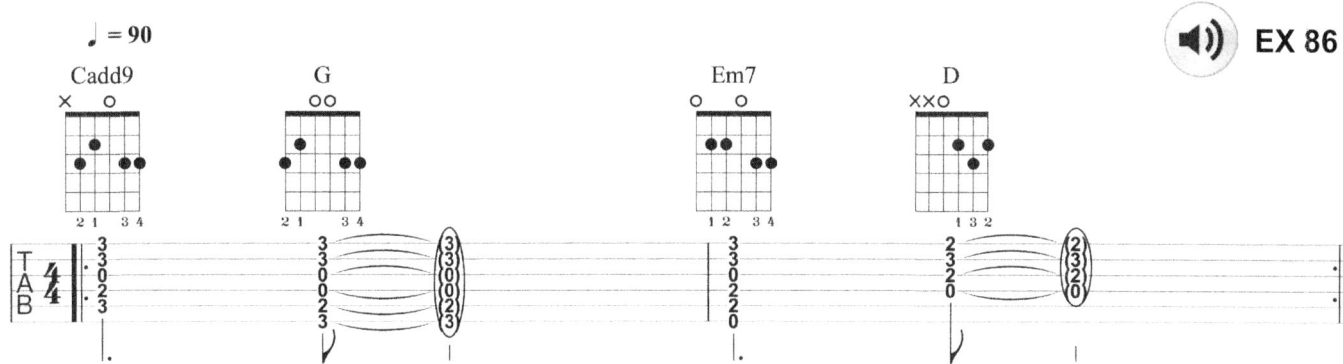

Notice that, by shifting the G and D chords over a half beat (to the "and" of beat 2), the energy level of the progression goes up. Why? Because the ear expects to hear these chord changes directly on beat 3 but, instead, they arrive a half-beat early. This phenomenon is sometimes referred to as *anticipation*, or a *push*, because the chords "anticipate" the change in harmony.

UNEXPECTED BEATS

Chord changes don't have to strictly occur on (or anticipate) beats 1 and 3. In fact, a fantastic way to spice up your chord progressions is to place a chord on an unexpected beat. One of my favorite rhythmic tricks is to place a chord change on beat 4, like this:

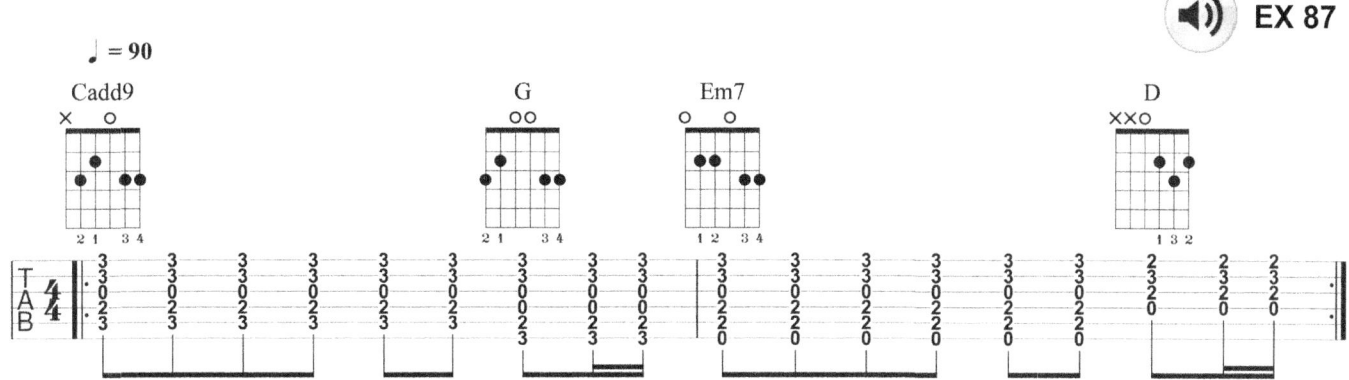

Notice how the driving eighth-note rhythm, paired with the chord changes on beat 4, helps to keep the energy level up and propel the music forward.

Chord changes can appear at an even faster clip than the examples we've worked on so far. In both classic and modern country music, as well as bluegrass, you'll hear songwriters place changes on every quarter note. One popular approach in country is to alternate bars of 3/4 and 4/4 time and place a chord change on each beat of the former, like this:

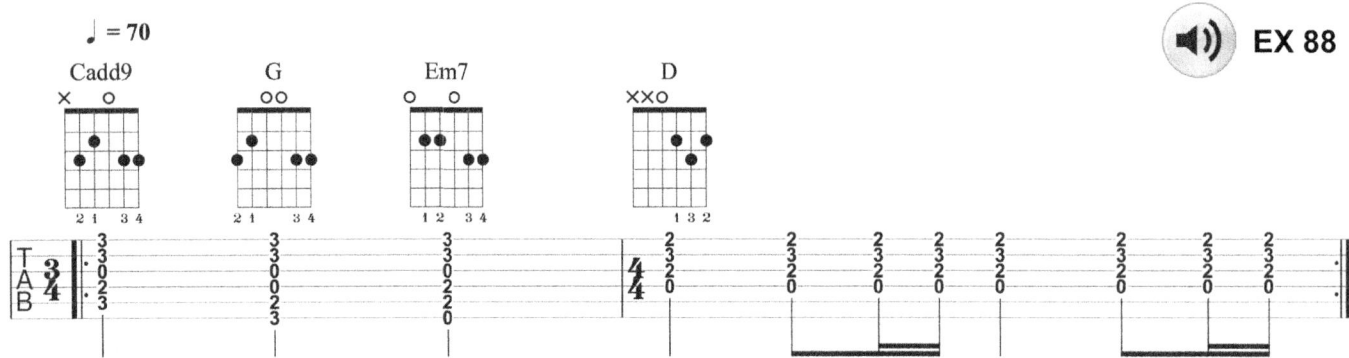
EX 88

One reason why this type of progression is so enduring is because the quick, quarter-note changes can be used to punctuate the vocal melody, which can be sung over the static one-chord harmony in measure 2. Conversely, the chord changes in measure 1 can serve as a catalyst for the vocal melody, and measure 2 can serve as a brief pause for lyrical reflection.

HARMONIC RHYTHM IN ROCK AND METAL

Rock and metal are a couple of music genres where harmonic rhythm is taken to the extreme. In these styles, chords sometimes last no longer than a half or quarter beat! In these situations, the objective is to create an overall tonality and vibe, rather than placing the focus on individual chords or chord cadences (resolution created by moving from one chord to another).

In the example below, our C–G–Em–D progression is played in a driving, syncopated eighth-note rhythm, with stripped-down root/5th power chords implying the chord changes. Notice that all four of the chords (C5, G5, E5, and D5) are crammed into one measure, with none lasting more than one beat. In cases like these, the song's key can become a little unclear, so use your ear to determine which chord sounds like the tonic (in this case, it's probably either G5 or D5, giving it a G major or D major/Mixolydian tonality).

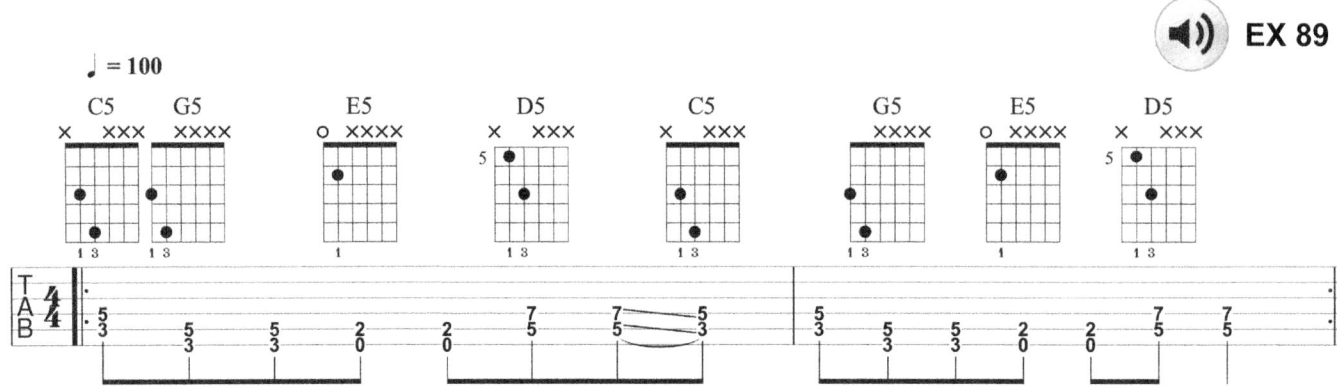
EX 89

The final example in this chapter is a metal riff in which the chords mostly appear for only a quarter beat (16th note) at a time and are offset by palm mutes of the low-E string. Again, the harmonic rhythm is extremely fast, but the main goal of a progression/riff like this is to create an overall vibe and tonality—in this case, E minor—not to place emphasis on specific major or minor chords.

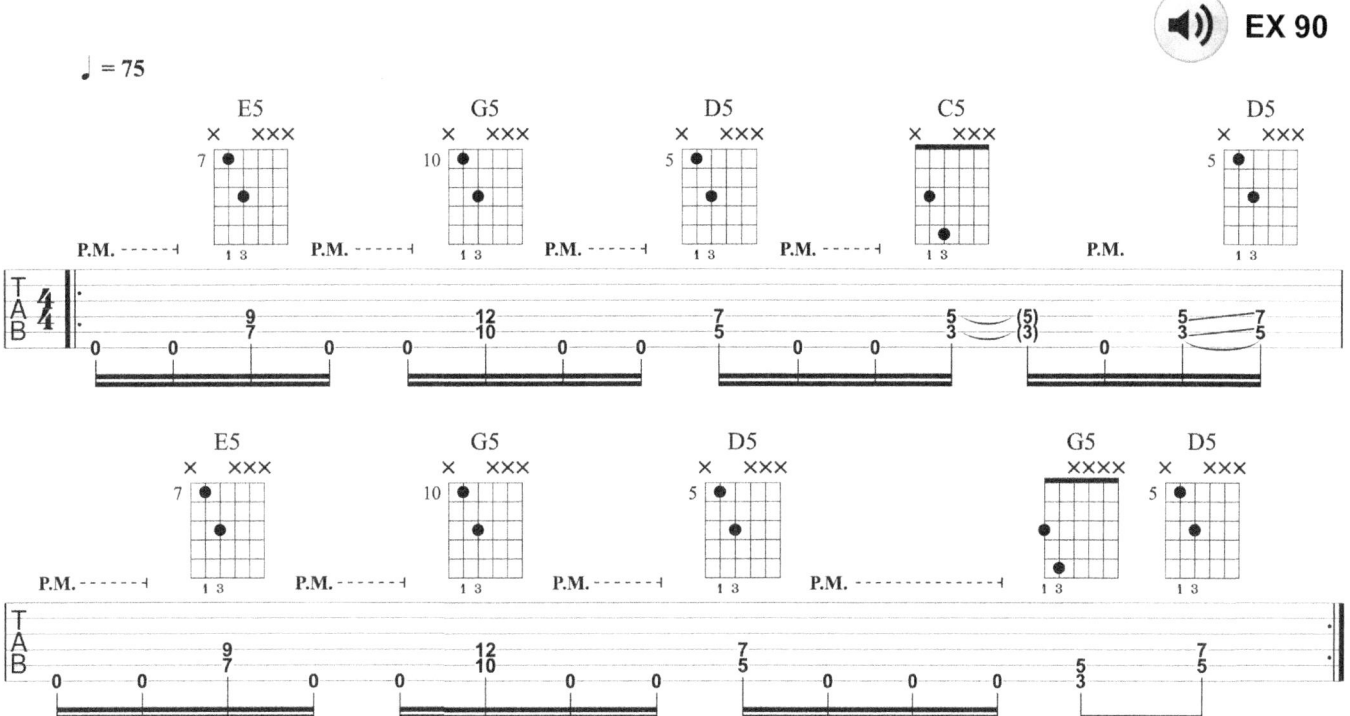

SECTION 3: WRITING PARTS TO FIT THE SONG

When it comes to songwriting on guitar, you're typically faced with two options: 1) you can create something completely new and compose the rest of the song around your new guitar creation, or 2) you can construct a guitar part to fit a song that you've started on another instrument, whether it's a drum groove, piano melody, or lyric.

Whatever the case may be, the important thing is to strive for continuity in your arrangement. In other words, if you've come up with a killer reggae groove on your guitar, then you're going to want the rest of the instrumentation (and lyric) to incorporate the styles of that genre. For example, a metal drum groove might not be the best option for a reggae rhythm guitar part. Similarly, if you've started a lyric about the modernization of Western society, then a pop ballad might not be the right feel.

Of course, there are exceptions to this rule. In fact, blending multiple genres to come up with new sounds has been going on for decades—even centuries. Nonetheless, you should always strive for cohesiveness in your arrangements. Sometimes genre-mixing works really well; other times, it can be a train wreck. If something sounds completely "out of left field," listeners will most likely find it difficult to stay tuned it.

The best approach, of course, it to use your ears and follow your instincts. If it sounds good to you, then it probably is good. With that in mind, the next five chapters are devoted to helping you create guitar parts that fit your song.

CHAPTER 12: GENRE-SPECIFIC GUITAR PARTS

In this chapter, we're going to learn how to turn basic chord progressions into guitar parts for several different music genres. After all, progressions are not exclusive to any one musical style; on the contrary, the songwriter has complete liberty to decide how the chord changes are going to sound.

BALLADS

Let's start with one of the simplest—and most popular—chord progressions: the I–IV–V. In the key of G, it looks like this:

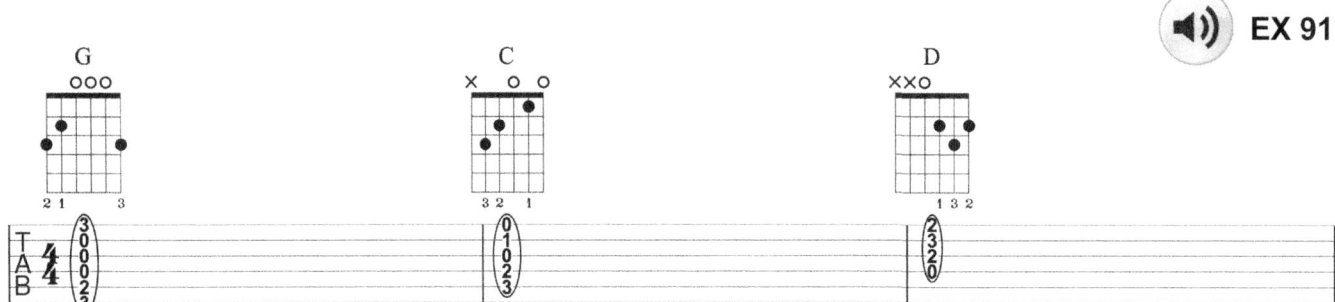

EX 91

Let's say you came up with a lyric that would sound great as a ballad. The first thing you should do is think about what musical elements define a ballad and how you can translate them to guitar. The most obvious characteristic of ballads is their slow tempo. Another characteristic is their emotional content, and one way to bring out the emotion of a song with a simple chord progression is to play it with a 6/8 meter.

Here's our G–C–D progression played as a 6/8 ballad:

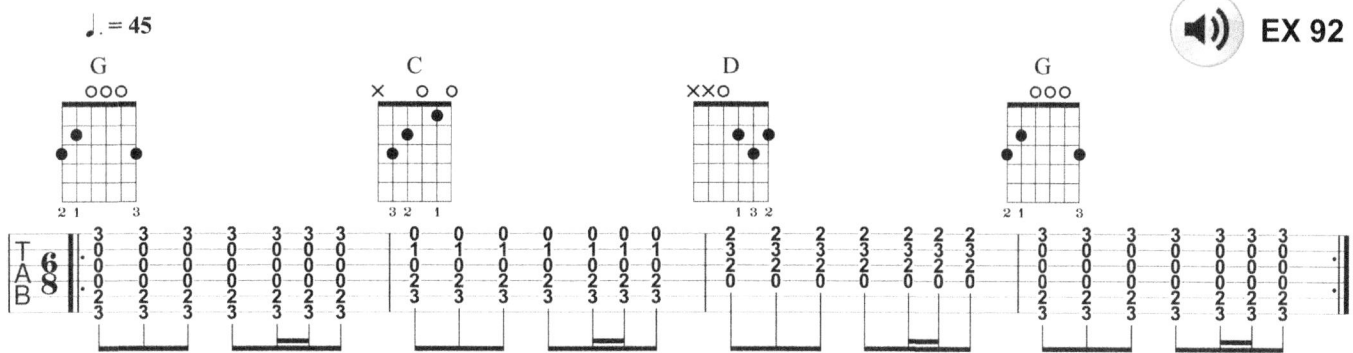

That works pretty nicely. If you really want to ramp up the emotional content, try adding a minor chord to the progression. Two good choices for our progression are Em or Am.

Here's how our progression sounds when substituting Em for the G chord in measure 4:

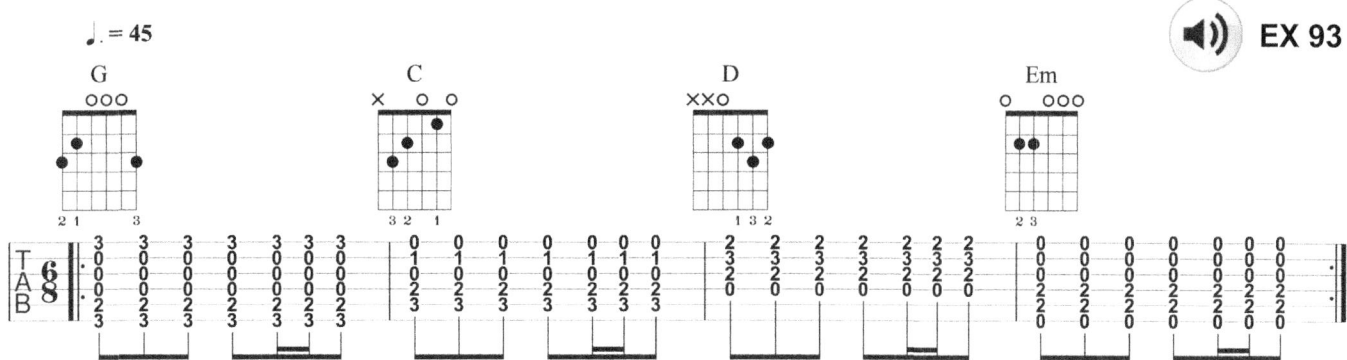

55

FUNK

Now let's take our G–C–D progression and come up with a guitar part for a funk tune. As we did with the ballad, spend a moment to think about what elements define a funk song. A couple that quickly come to mind are the syncopated 16th-note rhythms and extended chords, particularly dominant 7ths and 9ths.

With that in mind, let's transform our major triads into dominant 7th chords and play them in a syncopated 16th-note rhythm:

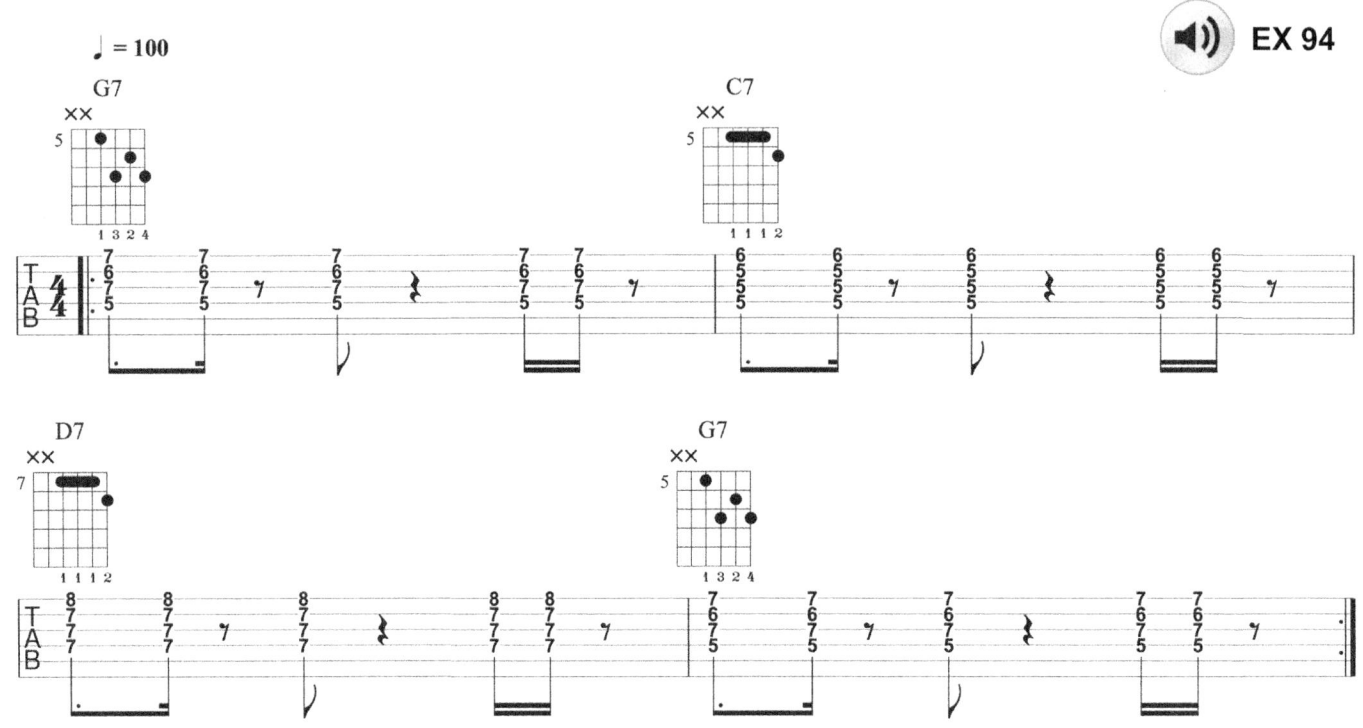

We can also add some scratch chords to really funk it up:

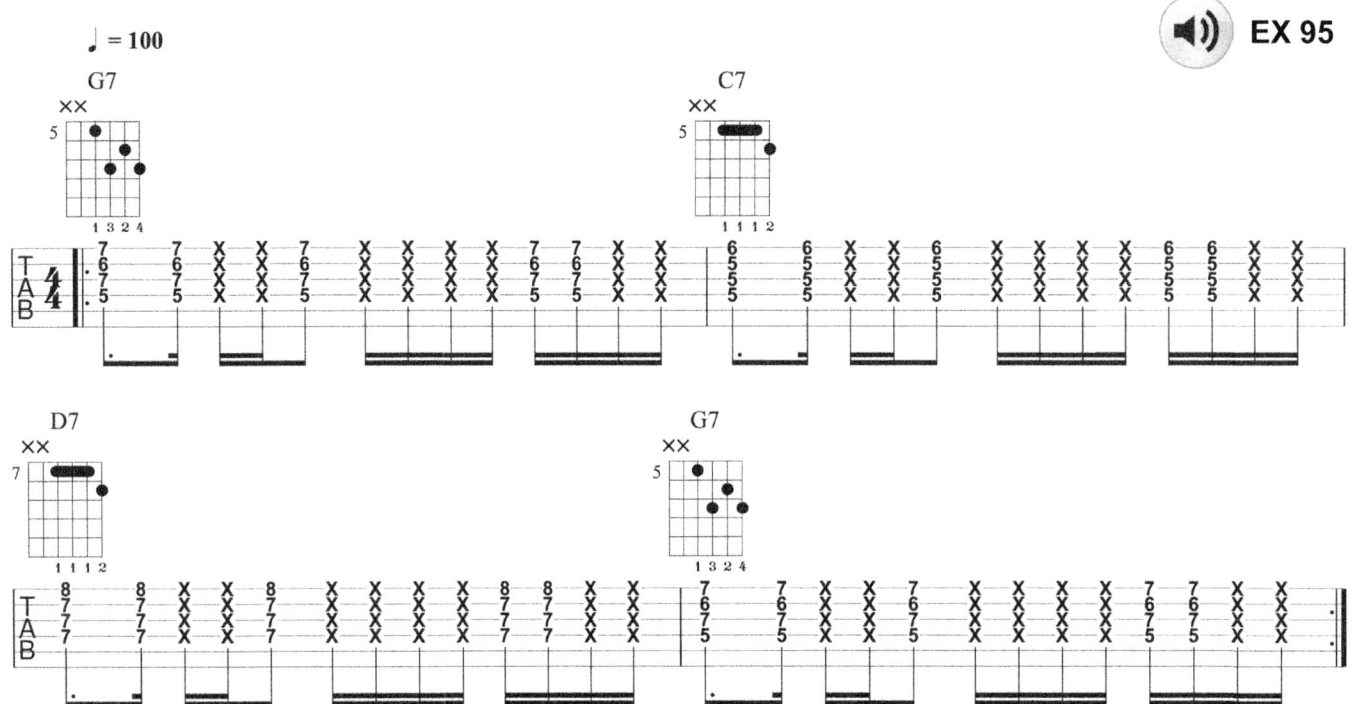

POP

Now let's turn our I–IV–V progression into a pop song by using the 10th intervals that we covered in chapter 10:

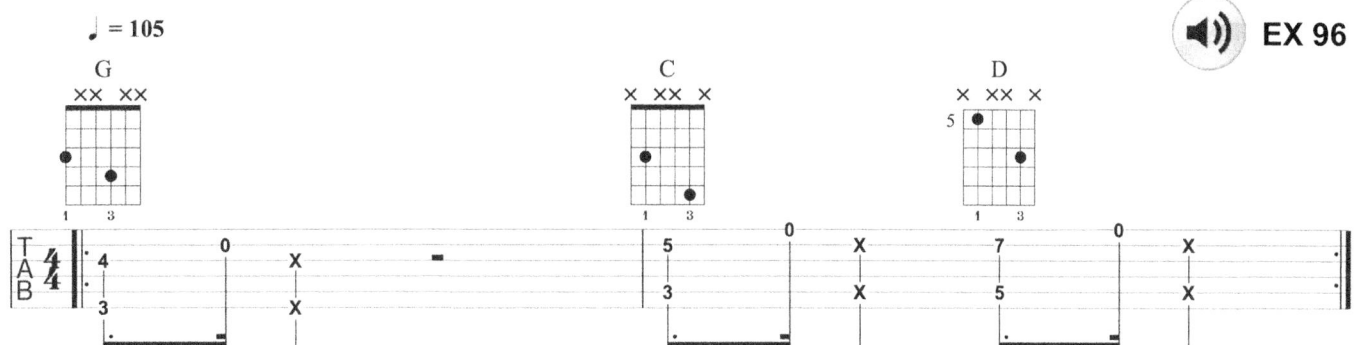

There are a few things going on in that example that are characteristics of pop guitar, including the use of space (notice how sparse the chords are), the percussive hits on beats 2 and 4 to mimic the snare drum, and the melodic open-string accents, which add a little ear candy.

MINOR CHORDS

Now let's introduce a minor chord to our three major triads. As we heard in our ballad example, minor chords are a great way to reduce some of the brightness and happiness of your chord progressions. Adding a minor chord doesn't necessarily mean the progression is now in a minor key; instead, it's a way to change the overall color, or vibe, of the chords.

Let's add the iii chord, Bm, to our G–C–D progression. Although it doesn't get the same attention as the ii chord or vi chord (Am and Em in the key of G, respectively), the iii chord adds an ear-pleasing sound that is both slightly unpredictable and a nice alternative to the other two minor chords. In addition to adding the Bm (iii) chord, let's switch up the order of the chords a bit to give us a I–V–iii–IV progression: G–D–Bm–C.

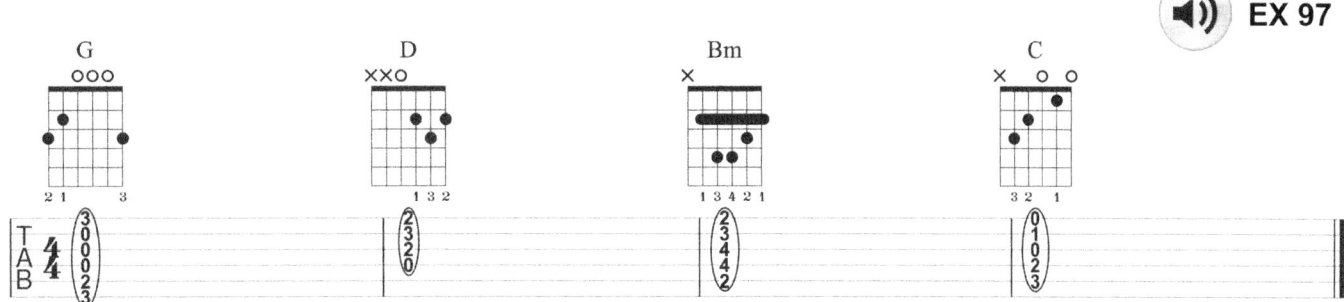

By adding just that one chord (iii), we've created a sound that is considerably different from that of our G–C–D progression.

Now that we have a new progression, G–D–Bm–C, let's use it to create some more genre-specific guitar parts. For example, we could compose a reggae "skank" by simply playing the chords as triads on the treble strings and in short, staccato fashion on beats 2 and 4, like this:

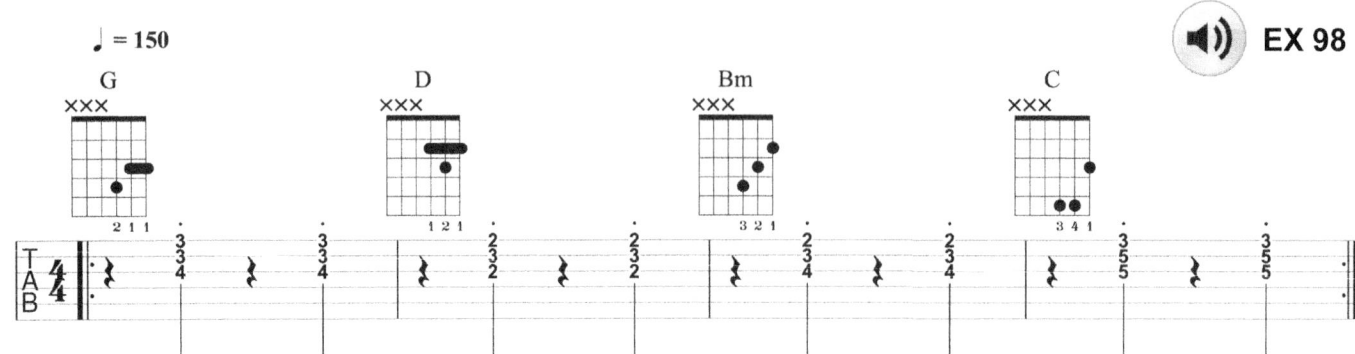

We could also take these same chord voicings, change up the rhythm a bit, and create a ska part:

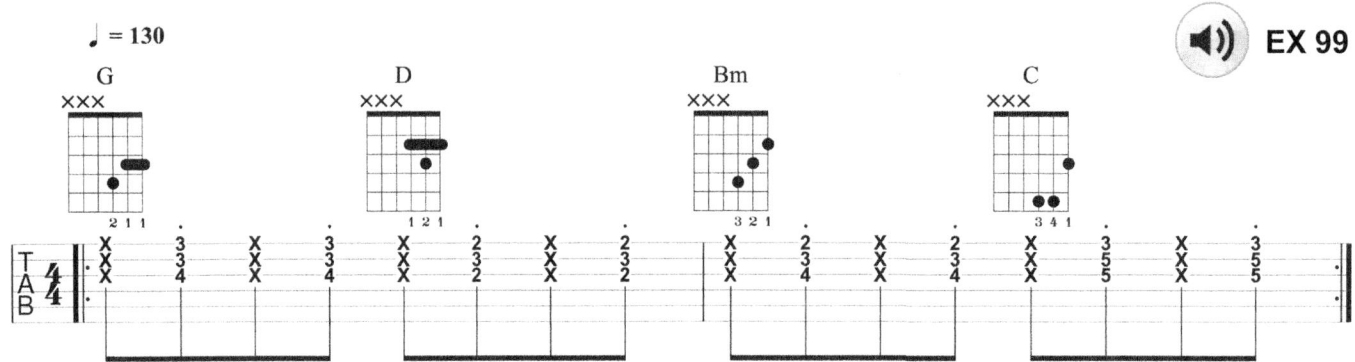

What I'm trying to instill in you is that chord progressions are akin to a collection of colors, and it's up to you decide what kind of portrait you're going to paint. You just need the right tools—in our case, the knowledge of what elements comprise the various music genres. This will enable you to write the songs you're hearing in your head.

MINOR PROGRESSIONS

Let's finish out this chapter with a minor *progression*, which is a great tool to have at your disposal, because sometimes you'll want a set of chords that is darker and moodier than what a major-key progression can provide. The progression below is similar to our previous one but, instead of the key of G, this progression is in the key of B minor. We know this because the progression *starts* on Bm and all of the chords belong to the Bm chord family (notice that A is substituted for C in this progression).

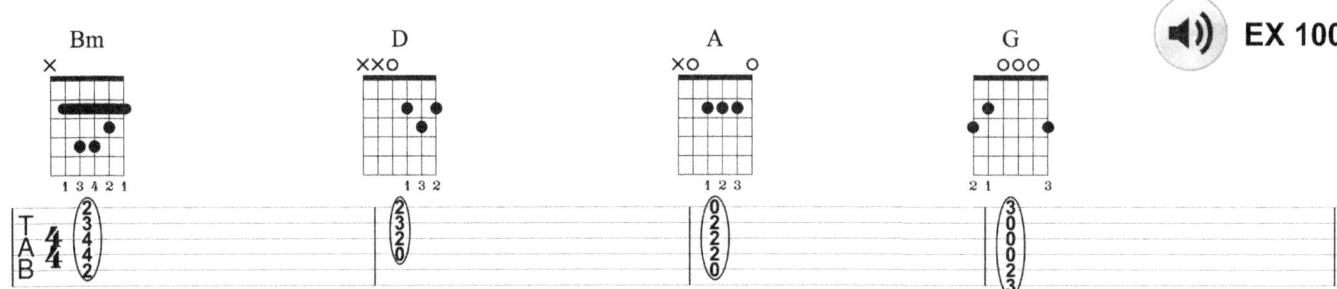

This progression, i–III–VII–VI (Bm–D–A–G), works well for palm-mute pop-punk riffs in the style of Green Day, Blink 182, Machine Gun Kelly, and Yungblud. To hear for yourself, check out the riff below:

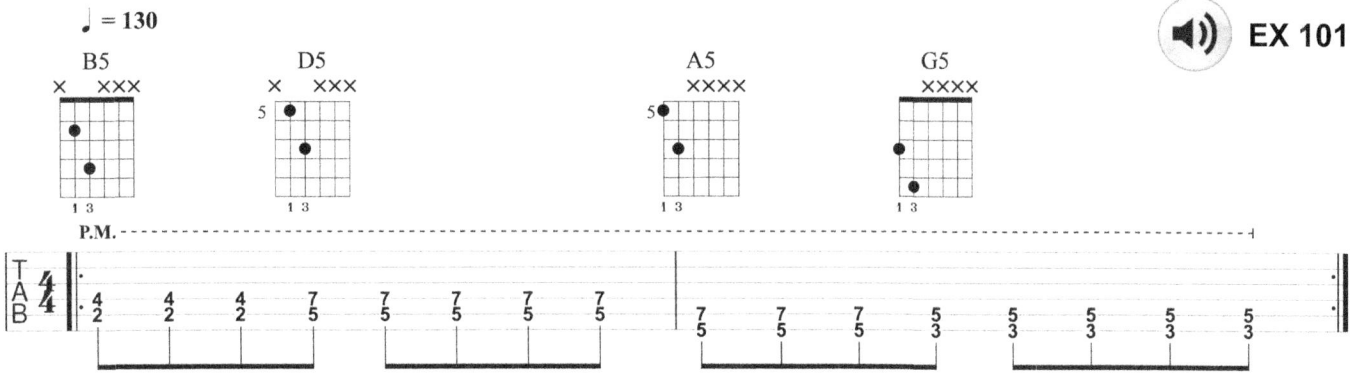

EX 101

Notice that our major and minor triads are stripped down to root/5th power chords and the subtle use of syncopation on the "and" of beat 2 in each measure. These, along with the palm-muting, are hallmarks of the pop-punk style.

We can also take this minor-key progression and add some chord embellishment to create some interesting country/folk-rock guitar parts, like this one:

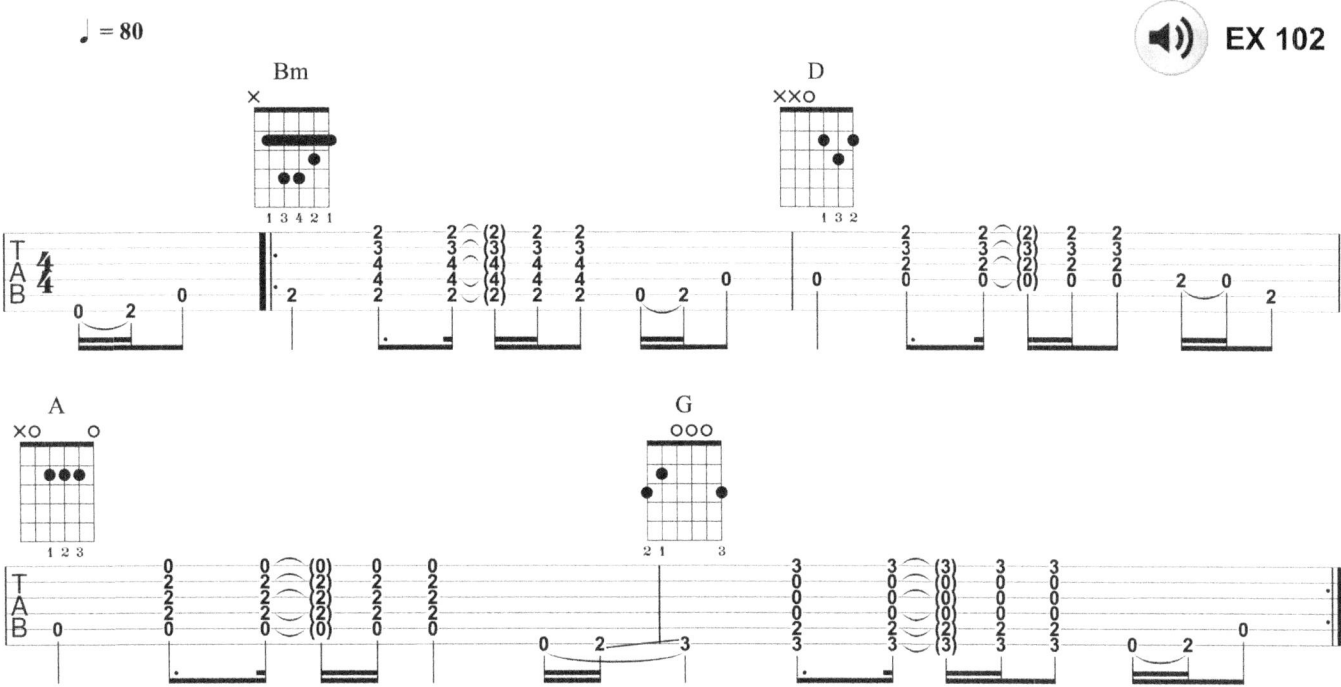

EX 102

As a songwriter or composer, you should study and learn as many chord progressions as you can. The best way to do this is to listen to music… *a lot* of it! While you're doing it, pull up the guitar tabs, most of which are available online for free. That way, you can follow along as you listen to how the chords color the song. And make sure not to limit your listening to one or two styles. On the contrary, branch out to other genres, as well. If you're a pop songwriter, try listening to EDM. If you're a country writer, try listening to pop or classical. Incorporating elements from other genres is what keeps music fresh and evolving—and what grabs listeners' attention! And while you're listening, make note of the musical elements that define the different genres, particularly the guitar. Then the next time you sit down to write, see if you can incorporate some of these new progressions and elements into your own compositions.

CHAPTER 13: PICKING A KEY

When writing a song, sometimes the key will come naturally and not a lot of thought has to go into; other times, outside factors have to be considered. For example, will this be a vocal track? If so, what's the vocal range of the singer? Further, what's the musical style? If it's rock or metal, you'll probably want to incorporate palm-muting on the low-E or A string, which considerably narrows your key choices. In this chapter, we'll discuss some of the factors that must be considered when choosing the right key for your song.

WRITING FOR VOCALS

Let's start with the elements that were mentioned in the introduction. First, when writing a song for vocals, you'll need to be cognizant of the melodic range; that is, what are the highest and lowest notes of the melody? Next, you'll need to determine whether the vocalist will be comfortable in this range. Will he/she struggle to hit the highest and lowest pitches? If the singer is yet to be determined, then pick a key that falls somewhere in the middle. If you or your co-writers have an "average" range, which is one to one-and-a-half octaves, and are comfortable singing the melody, then it should be fine for most vocalists.

If you're writing a song that will feature open-chord strumming—for example, a country, folk/rock, or Americana tune—then you can start with a common open-position key like G, C, or D. Let's say you come up with a progression like the one below (a I–IV–I–V in the key of C):

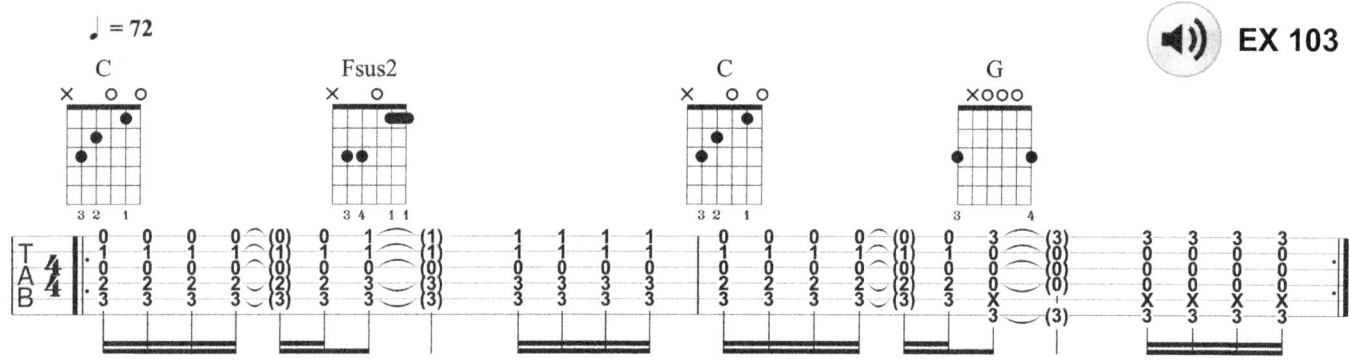

EX 103

You could start to write you melody around this progression, but if some of the notes feel too high or too low, you could simply change the key. The great thing about writing songs on guitar with open chords is that all you need to do to change keys is add a *capo*, a device that clamps onto the neck to shorten the length of the strings and raise their pitch.

After applying the capo, experiment with different keys, moving it up and down the neck until the melodic range feels most natural. Even though the pitch of the strings continues to go higher as you move the capo up the neck, the melody doesn't necessarily have to follow the same trend. In fact, as you move the capo up the neck to change keys, you can start to drop down an octave some of the higher pitches that gave you trouble. Similarly, some of the lower melody notes that gave you trouble will start to move higher in pitch as you slide the capo further up the neck.

For example, let's say this is the melody you wrote for your C–Fsus2–C–G progression:

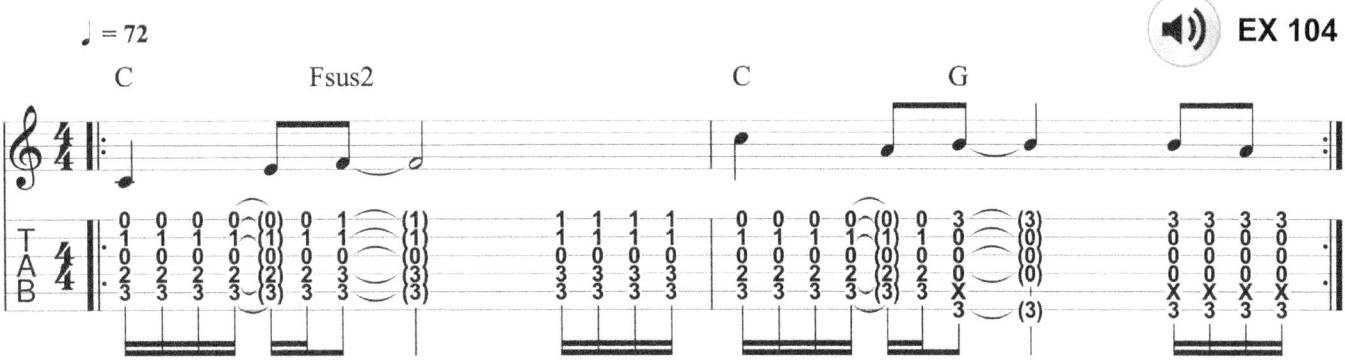

For most vocalists, the pitches in measure 1 are manageable; however, the pitches in measure 2 will be out of the range of most singers, particularly male vocalists. The solution is to slide the capo up the neck and find a key where all the notes fit comfortably in a range suitable for most singers. For example, let's take our previous chord progression, C–Fsus2–C–G, and play the same voicings but with the capo at fret 4 (capoed fret is "0" in tab), which will put us in the key of E.

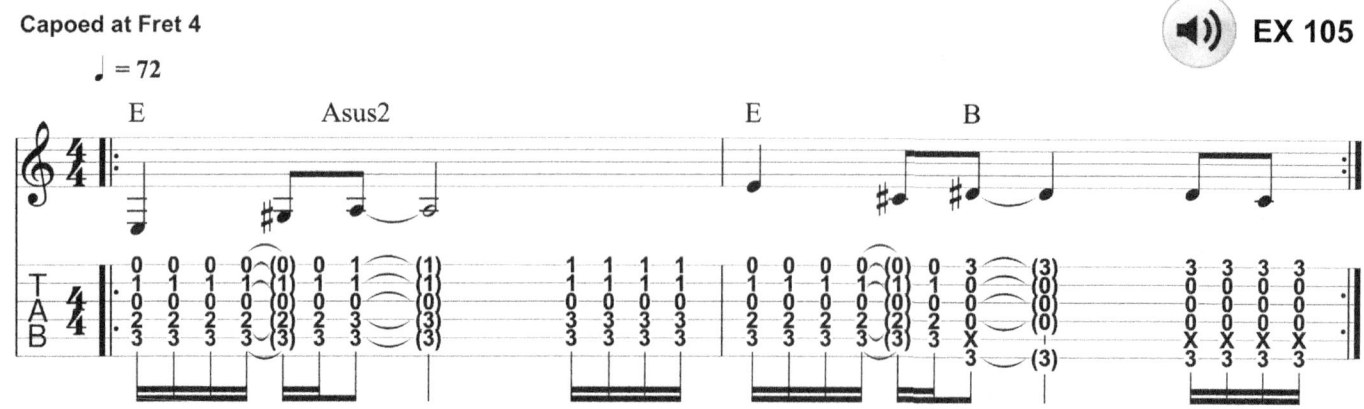

Notice that the higher pitches in measure 2 are now in a more comfortable register, and the melody as a whole is in a more accommodating range for a majority of singers. As we shifted the capo up a major 3rd (two whole steps, or four frets), we transposed our melody and progression from C to E; however, the melody, if sung as written, would've been way too high for everyone but Maria Carey and Ariana Grande. So, we dropped the melody down an octave. This goes back to what I mentioned earlier: even though the chords sound higher in pitch with the capo, the melody doesn't have to do the same. In other words, find the octave, whether it's lower or higher, that works for each note. You can even try jumping from higher to lower octave, or vice versa, in your melodies to add dynamics.

You can treat barre chords like capoed open chords, as well. In other words, if you come up with a cool riff or progression that uses barre chords exclusively (i.e., no open strings), then you can simply shift the chords up or down the fretboard to find a key that works best for your song/melody. For example, let's say you come up with the following riff, which is based on a I–V–iii–IV (E–B–G♯m–A) progression in E:

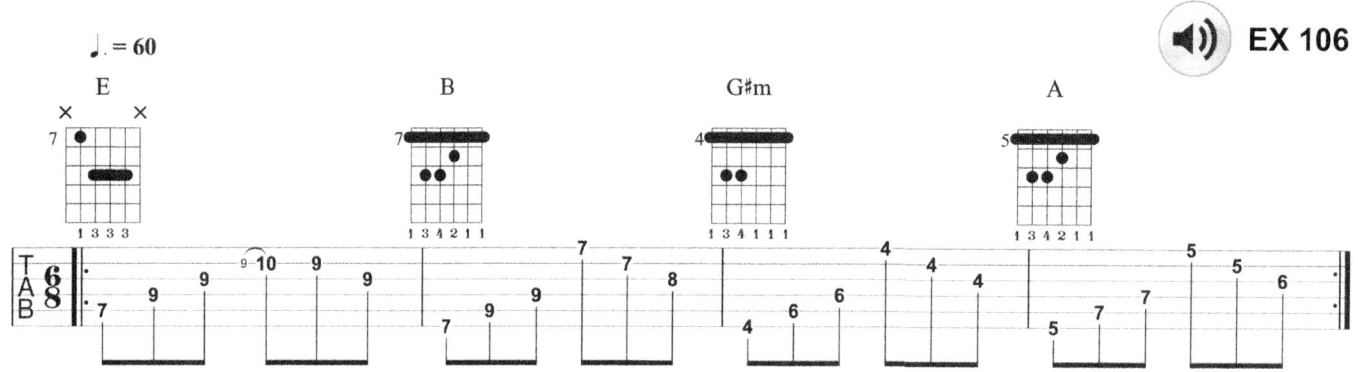

You think the riff sounds great as written, but it doesn't fit the vocal range of your singer, or perhaps you just don't like the vibe of the key, E major. After all, every key has its own "color," and sometimes certain keys just feel better than others in certain situations. This is because each pitch is based on a frequency; the lower the pitch, the lower the frequency, and the higher the pitch, the higher the frequency.

Collectively, the pitches of a key (i.e., the tonality) have a unique sound that make us feel a certain way. For example, low frequencies from a kick drum or bass make us want to move. Conversely, high frequencies stimulate the brain and make us more alert and give us energy. Therefore, by changing the key of a song, we're subtlety (or not so subtlety) changing the overall mood that it creates.

Let's try this with our E–B–G♯m–A riff. First, let's shift the chords up the neck five frets, or a perfect 4th, to hear how they sound in the key of A:

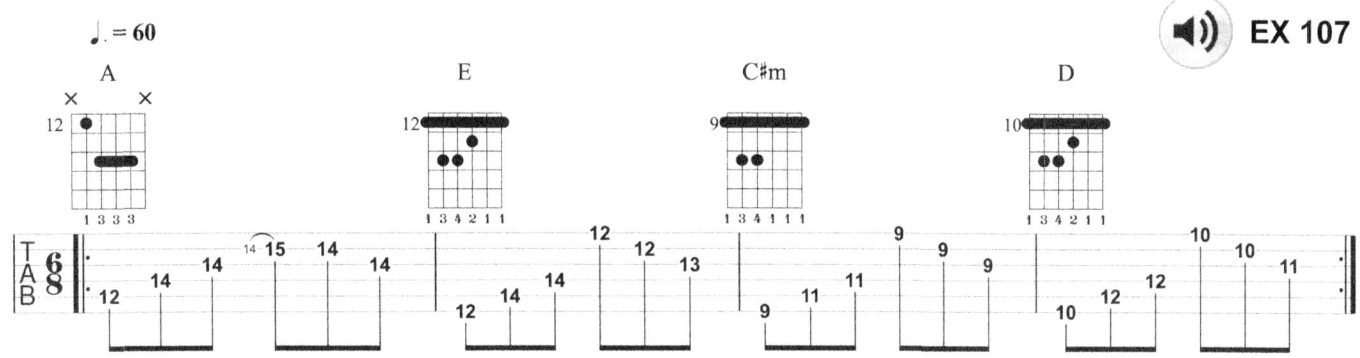

Sounds brighter and happier, right? Now let's play the same progression but with the I chord (A) and V chord (E) in the lower octave:

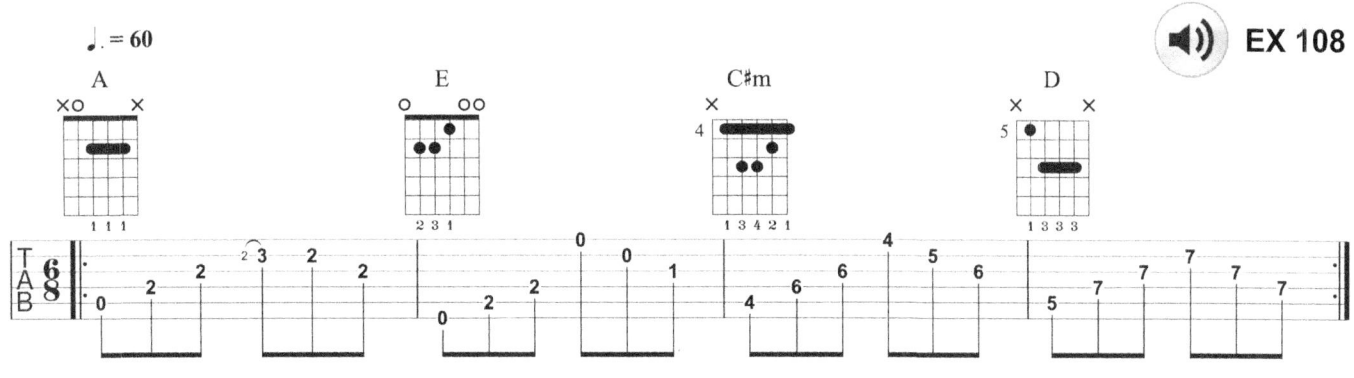

The lower octave imparts a slightly darker quality to the progression, as do the alternate C♯m and D chord voicings, which lack the highest notes of the original chords.

So, whether you're playing open chords or barre chords, be sure to experiment with various keys to find the one that best fits the vocal and overall vibe of your track. Heck, sometimes just moving one or two chords up or down an octave can open up a whole different sound, as demonstrated in our last example.

BASS-STRING INFLUENCE

No keys are more popular amongst guitar-playing composers and songwriters than E and A, and for obvious reasons: they're the two lowest strings on the instrument. When these two strings are palm-muted or allowed to ring open, they help to reinforce the song's tonal center (key) and provide extra heft to the low-end. Naturally, you'll frequently hear these two keys in rock and metal. Let's look at a few ways these two strings can help to influence your song's key.

In the example below, the open low-E string is allowed to ring open while two-note chords (dyads) are shifted along strings 4–5. I've included the implied harmony, E–F#m7–E–Emaj7sus2, above the tab staff, but the riff is really just one big E chord with some non-chord tones thrown in to give it some color and movement.

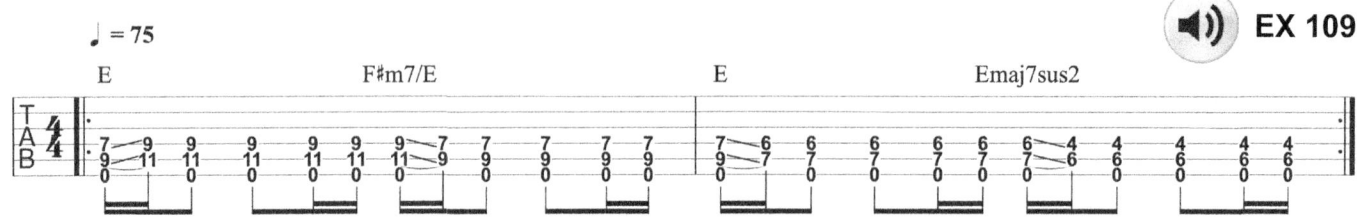

When using the open low-E string to imply or reinforce the song's key, we're not relegated to E major; on the contrary, some pretty cool E *minor* riffs can be created, as well. For example, let's take or previous E major riff and make it minor, which gives us this:

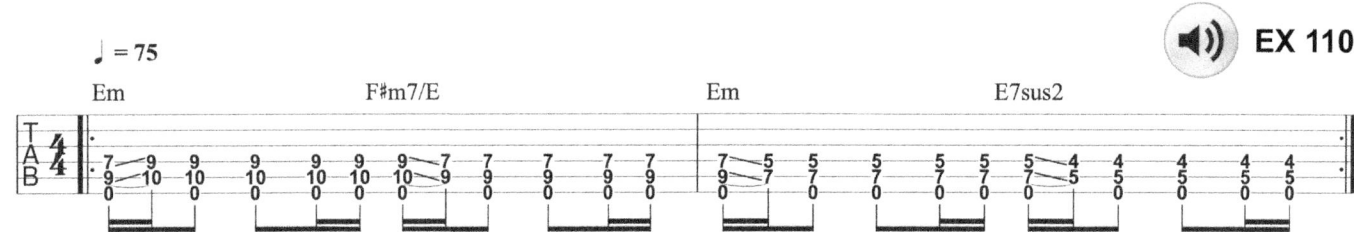

By adjusting just a few notes, we're able to convert our E major idea to E minor, which results in a much darker-sounding riff, perfect for rock or metal applications.

Palm-muted riffs work in much the same way. Let's start with an E major riff that juxtaposes power chords, major dyads, and palm-mutes of the low-E string:

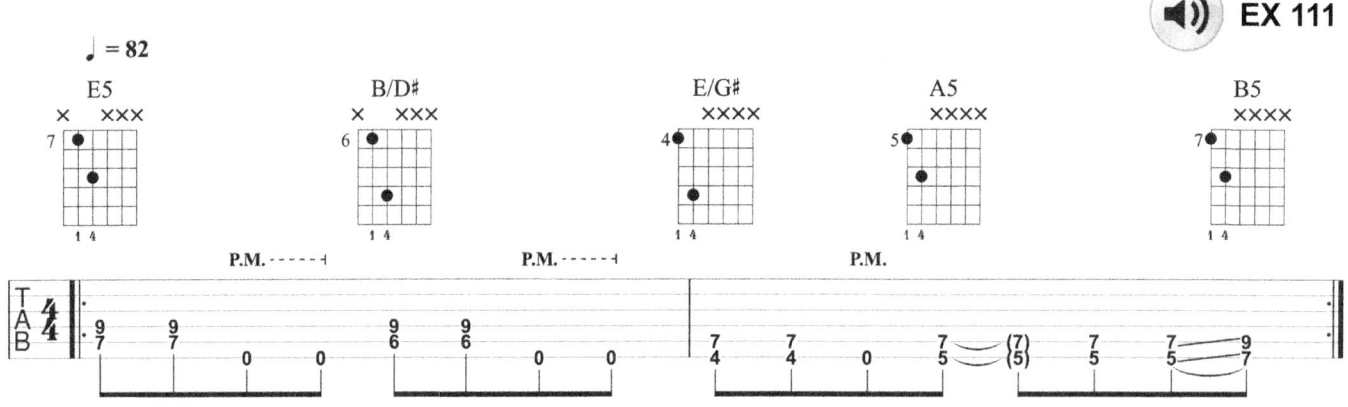

Compared to our E minor riff, notice how much brighter this riff sounds, and also note how the palm-mutes reinforce the E major tonality.

Now let's create a similar riff but in the key of E *minor*. Our next example uses the same palm-muting as in the previous example but substitutes a few new chords (C5, G5, and D/F#) to create the E minor tonality.

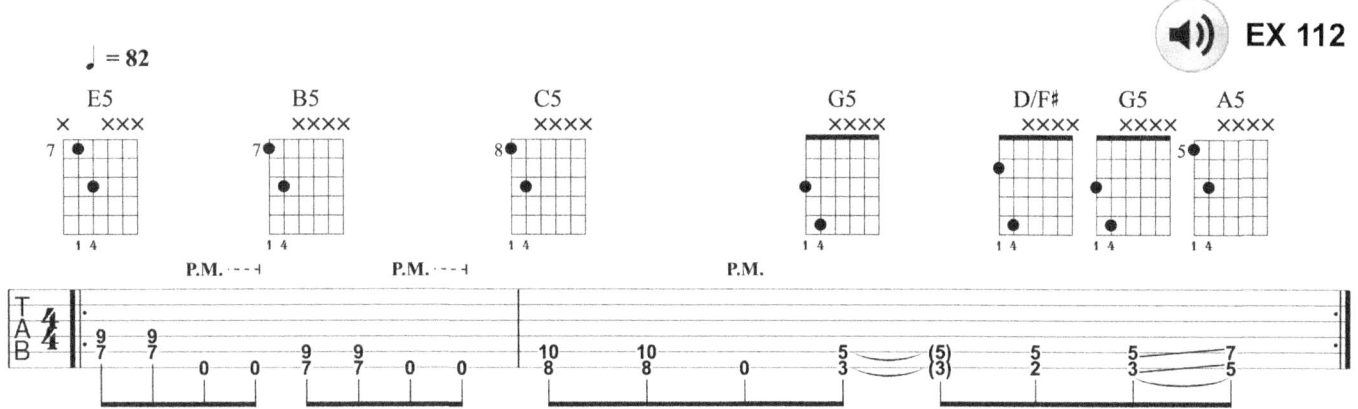

Again, notice how the palm-muting hammers home the riff's key—in this case, E minor—and how the new chords lend a moodier quality to the overall sound.

We can create similar riffs with the open A string, as well, and use it to drive home the song's key, whether major or minor. Below is an uptempo riff that alternates the open A string and fretted pitches along string 4, all of which are derived from the A major scale (A–B–C♯–D–E–F♯–G♯). Not a single chord is struck but, because of the droning open A string, combined with the fretted pitches, the key of the song, A major, is firmly established.

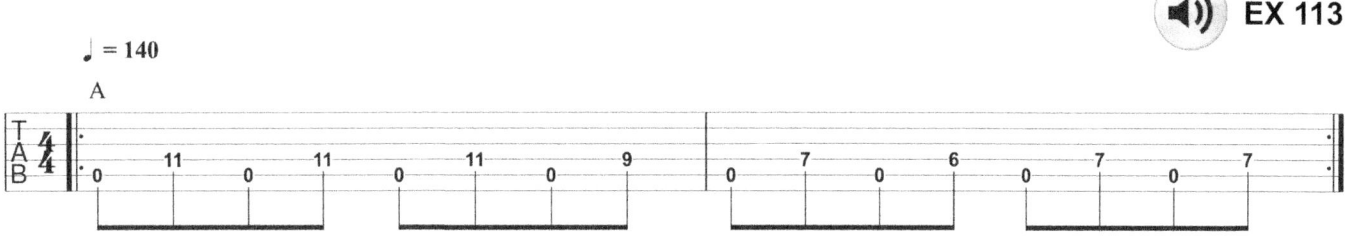

Now, for the sake of thoroughness, below is the same riff but played in the key of A *minor*—harmonic minor to be exact. Again, notice the darker quality.

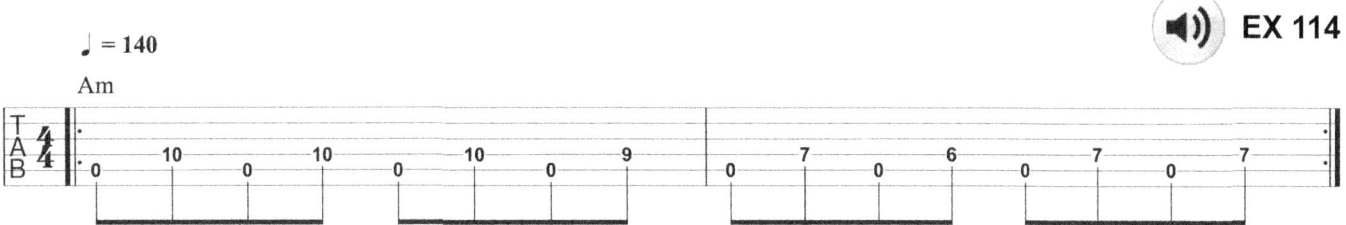

You can use a capo on these types of riffs to change keys, as well, but be aware that you start to lose some of the low-end impact the further up the neck you go. After all, the reason guitarists love to compose in these two keys (E and A) is because of the sonic punch the open strings provide.

CHAPTER 14: MAJOR OR MINOR?

Deciding whether your song should be in a major or minor key basically boils down to personal preference and what your song calls for. Major chords sound "bright" and "happy," whereas minor chords sound "dark" and "sad." That said, when constructing chord progressions, some major progressions can sound slightly dark, even minor, while certain minor progressions can sound almost major in quality. Much of this depends on the melody and instrumentation of the song, of course, but determining which chords to select for your song's progression, as well as deciding the order in which to play them, is an important topic worthy of a deep dive. Let's get started…

THE I–V–vi–IV PROGRESSION

In this chapter, we're going to experiment with a couple of popular four-chord progressions by rearranging the order of the chords to hear how different sequences sound, including how you can easily turn a major progression into a minor one. Our first progression, I–V–vi–IV, is arguably the most popular in all of music; it's heard in everything from pop and rock to country and folk. Played in the key of G, the progression is G–D–Em–C:

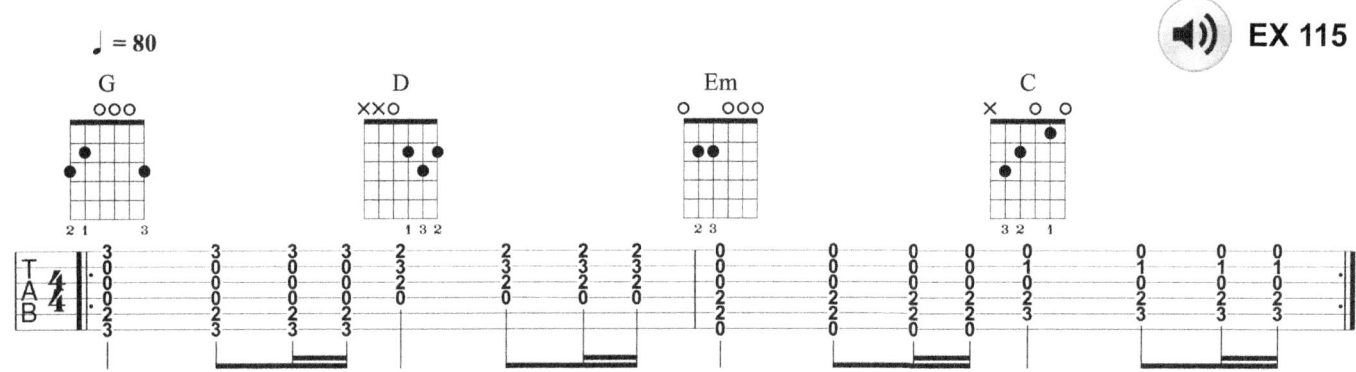

This major progression might not sound "happy," but it does have a rather bright, hopeful quality to it. Now let's rearrange a couple of chords and hear how it sounds. Below is a G–C–Em–D (I–IV–vi–V) progression—the same progression as our previous example, only the C and D chords have been switched. Notice that, by moving from G to C, rather than from G to D, the overall sound of the progression is slightly darker.

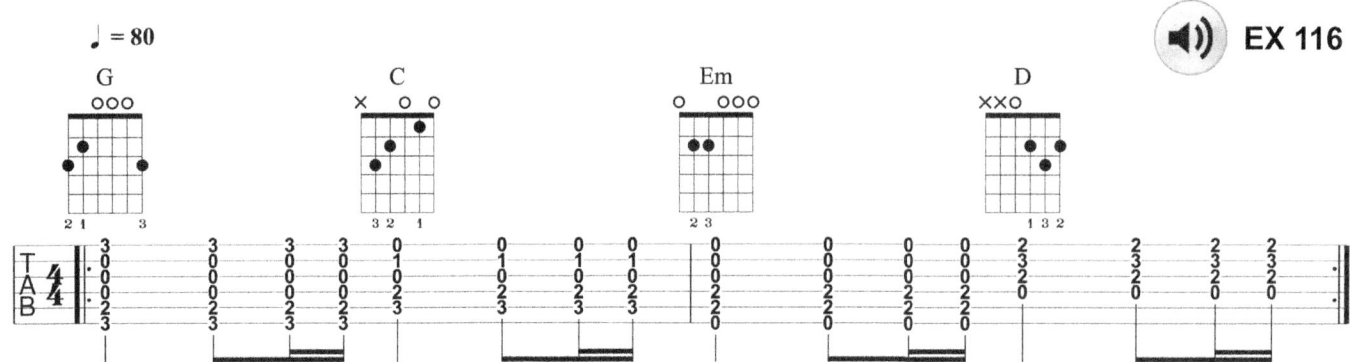

66

Now let's try starting on a chord other than the tonic, G, and hear how it sounds. Our next example features a V–vi–IV–I progression in G: D–Em–C–G. Again, the same four chords from our original progression are present, only now we're starting on the V chord, D.

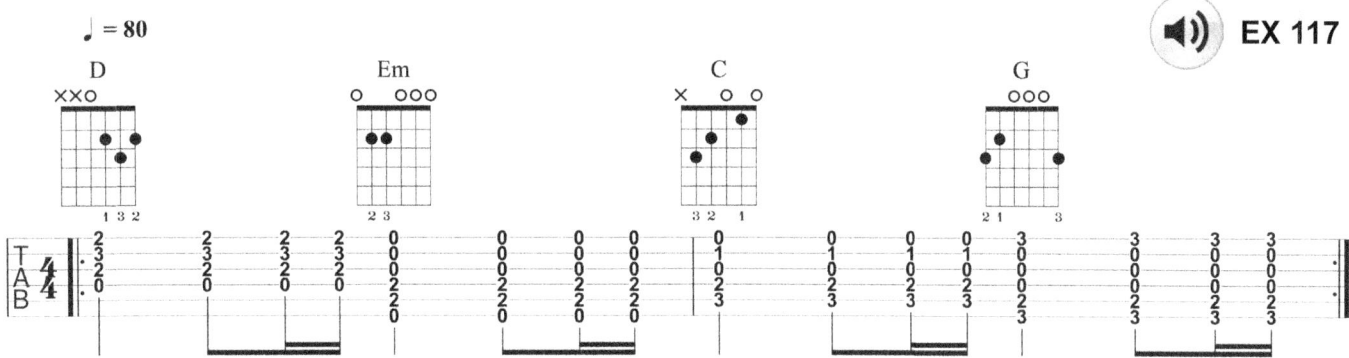

When a progression starts on a chord other than the tonic, the tonal center can be a little nebulous, but the main point here is the overall vibe of the progression and whether it's right or wrong for the song you're trying to write, so experiment and pay attention to how the progression makes you feel. Does it make you feel happy? Sad? Indifferent?

Now let's turn our major G–D–Em–C progression into a minor one. To accomplish this, we simply need to *start* on the sole minor chord, Em. For example, we could play an Em–C–G–D progression, which is identical to our previous progression, D–Em–C–G (V–vi–IV–I), only we're starting on Em instead of D.

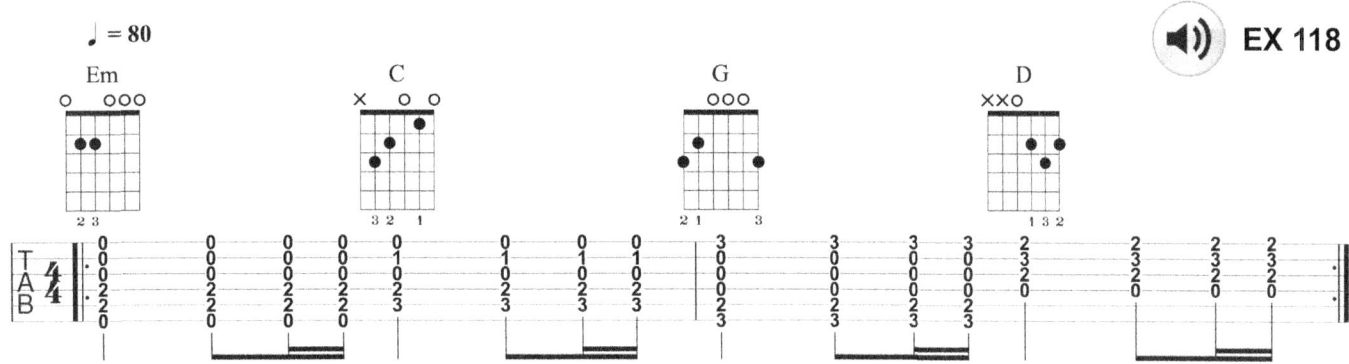

Notice that, even though we're playing the same chords, in the same order, as our previous progression, by starting on—and ultimately resolving to—Em, we're left with a slighter darker and moodier *minor* progression.

67

THE I–vi–ii–V PROGRESSION

Now let's switch keys and add another minor chord to even things out. The following chord changes, C–Am–Dm–G, are a I–vi–ii–V progression in the key of C major. This progression is often heard in jazz, but occasionally shows up in other music genres, as well, including pop. In addition to having an equal number of major and minor chords, the two minor chords, Am and Dm, are played back to back. As you play through the chord changes, make note of how they make you feel and what type of mood they set.

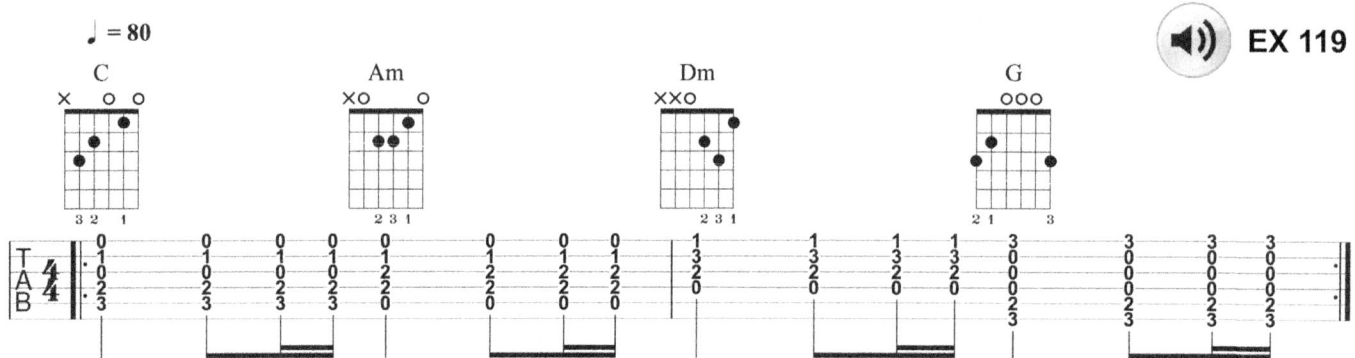

EX 119

Notice how the back-to-back minor chords imparts a distinct minor-key sound to an otherwise major-key progression (C). Now let's change up the order of these chords and see what kind of sound we can create. Our next set of changes is a I–ii–vi–V (C–Dm–Am–G) progression. It's identical to our previous progression, only the order of the minor chords, Am and Dm, has been reversed.

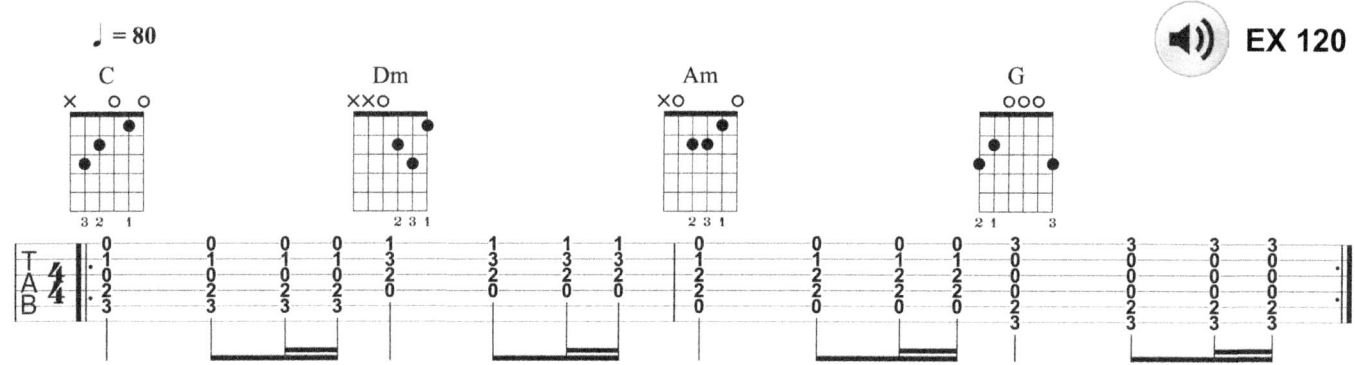

EX 120

This progression, like the previous one, has a darker quality to it due to the presence of two minor chords; however, the I–ii (C–Dm) change in measure 1 has a slightly brighter sound than the I–vi (C–Am) change of the previous progression.

Now let's experiment with starting our I–vi–ii–V progression with a chord other than the tonic, C. Our next progression is similar to the previous one, C–Dm–Am–G, only now we're starting on the V chord, G, and ending on the tonic, C.

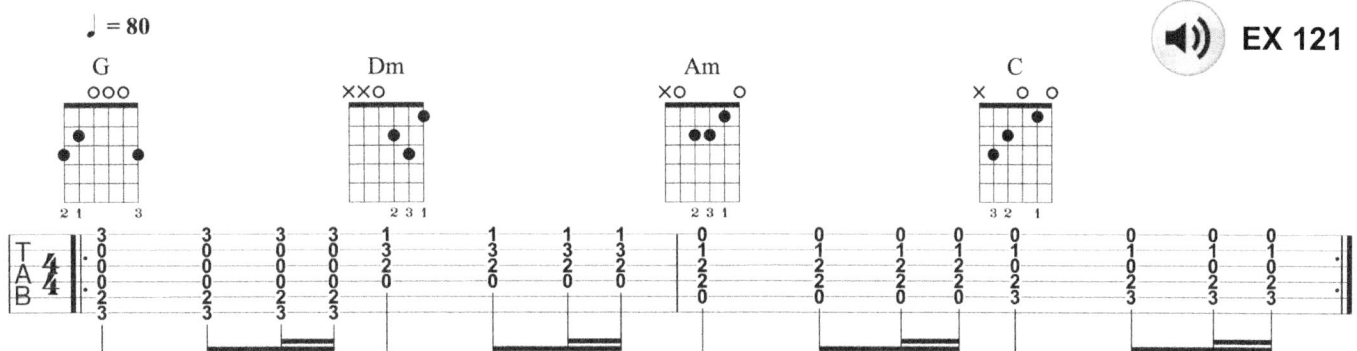

What do you think? To me, starting on the G chord and ending on C chord has a considerably brighter, happier sound compared to starting on C and ending on G.

Let's finish off this chapter by taking our major I–vi–ii–V changes and turning them into a wholly minor progression. The progression below, Am–Dm–C–G, features the same four chords that we've been working on, only now we're starting on—and resolving to—Am, thereby making it a *minor* progression.

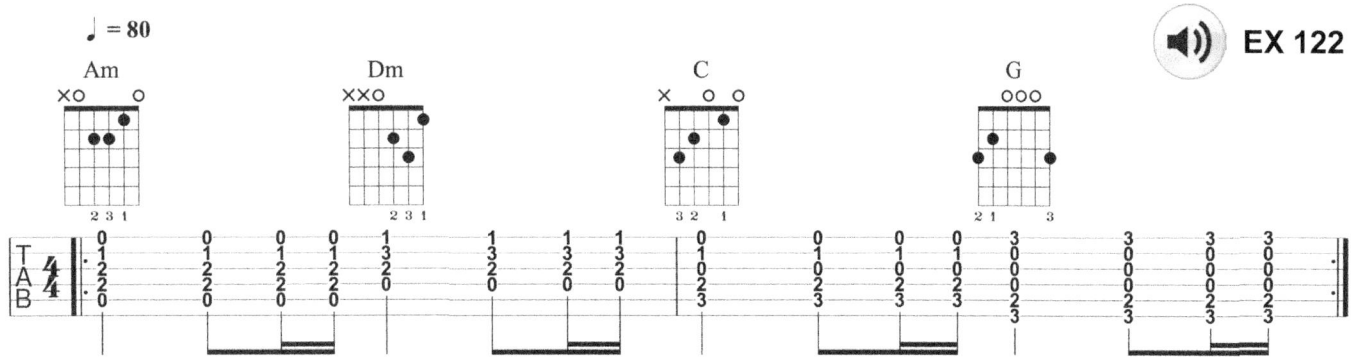

Now that we're in a minor key, you can really here the darker qualities, particularly the i–iv (Am–Dm) change in measure 1. However, the gloomier sound seems to carry over to measure 2, as well, despite the presence of two major chords, C and G. This is no doubt due to our ears and brain anticipating resolution to the Am chord.

CHAPTER 15: BUILDING GUITAR PARTS AROUND A BASS LINE

Sometimes, you might not be the one initiating a songwriting session. In fact, if you're a member of a band, you've probably been a part of a jam session where the bass player or drummer comes up with a killer groove that is the genesis of a song. In the next two chapters, we're going to discuss some approaches you can take to make your guitar parts fit a great bass line or drum groove. First up is the bass.

QUARTER-NOTE GROOVE

In this chapter, we're going to work with bass lines that get increasingly more complex as we go along. For starters, let's say your bass player comes up with the line shown below. The first thing you should pay attention to is the rhythm, because this will dictate how rhythmically complex your guitar part can (should) be.

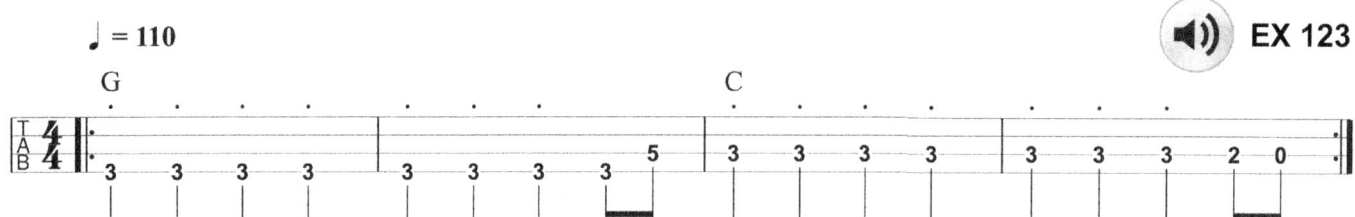

Since the bass line is predominantly staccato quarter notes, you can get pretty "busy" with your guitar part. Below is an idea that might work for this bass line. It follows the I–IV (G–C) chord change with triad inversions played up the neck and accomplishes a few things: 1) the eighth notes provide additional rhythmic energy and fill the gaps between the bass line's staccato quarter notes, 2) the higher range is a nice contrast to the low end of the bass, and 3) the arpeggiated chords create a counter-melody to the vocal. Nice!

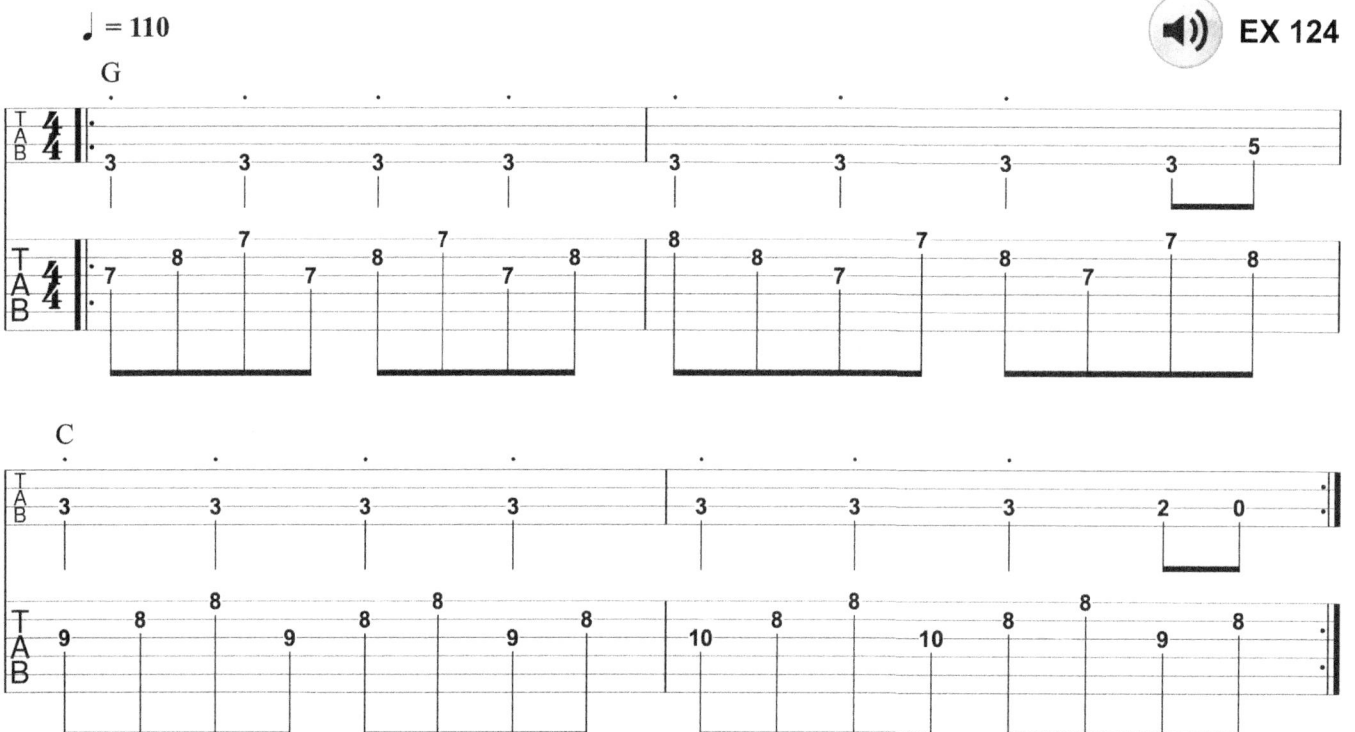

EIGHTH-NOTE GROOVE

Now let's try another bass line, one that's a little busier, rhythmically:

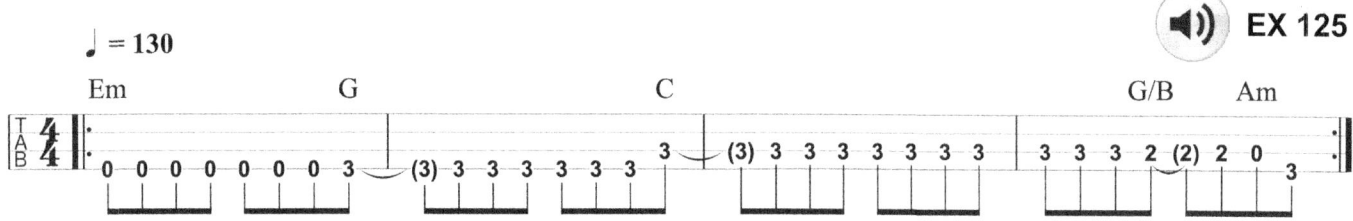

Because of the change in the rhythmic subdivision (from quarter notes to eighth notes), keeping the guitar part simple is a good idea. One approach is to play mostly quarter, half, and/or whole notes, like this:

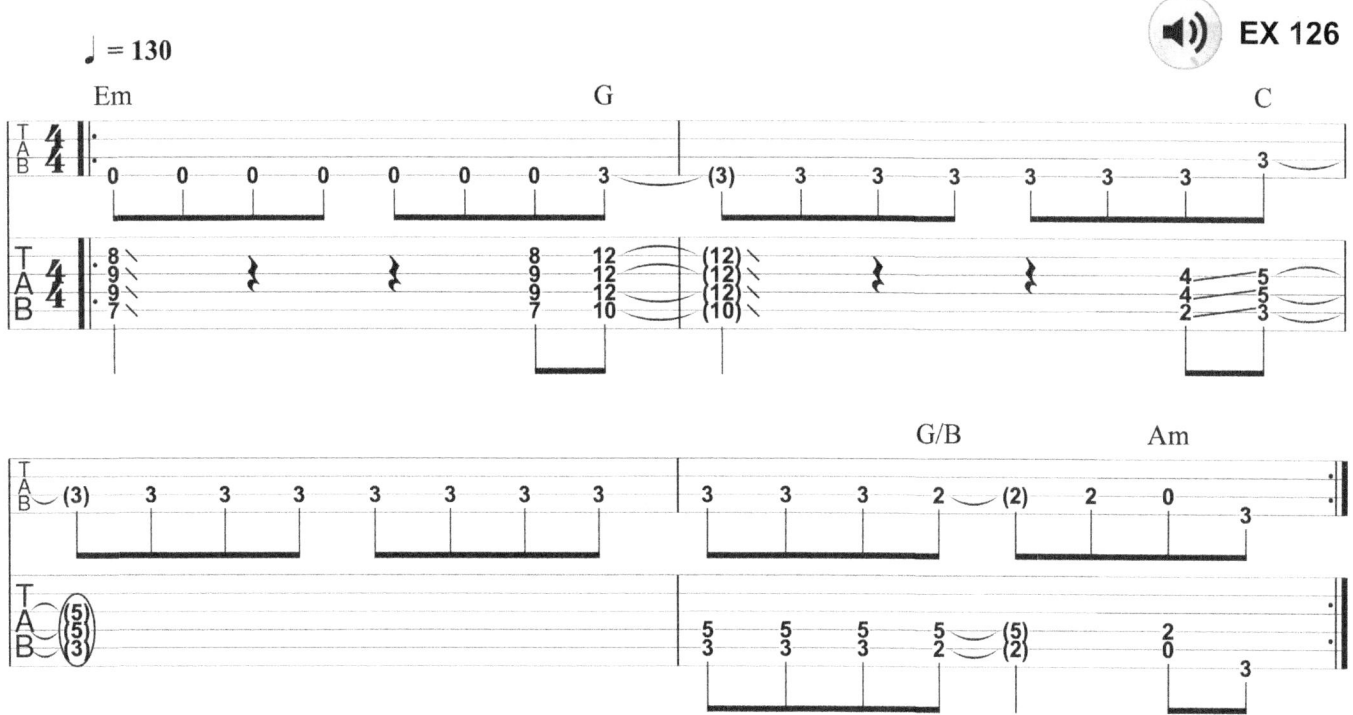

Notice how the guitar part is used to accent each chord change but, by adding rests (measures 1–2) and holding out chords (measure 3), it stays out of the way of the driving bass line. In other words, the guitar lets the bass take the spotlight. Then, in measure 4, the guitar plays in unison with the bass to signal a return to the top of the four-bar riff. Awesome!

REGGAE GROOVE

So far, our bass lines have been pretty straightforward, but that's not always the case. For example, if you play in a funk or reggae band—or you're trying to write a song in one of those styles—the bass grooves can get quite complex. Let's take a look at one example and then see what kind of guitar part might work with it.

The example below is reggae bass line that features a non-diatonic A–G–A–E (I–♭VII–I–V) progression and a slightly syncopated rhythm. Although the line mostly consists of quarter notes and eighth notes, the relatively fast tempo (160 BPM) creates more complexity.

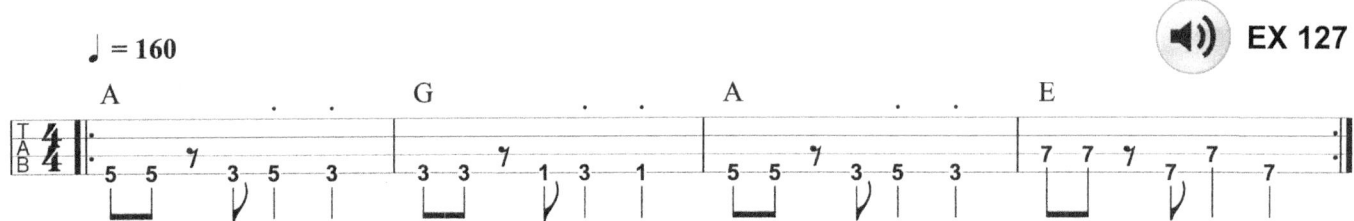

The best approach for this relatively busy groove is to either play in unison with the bass, which is a popular approach in reggae, or play a simple "skank" part, like this:

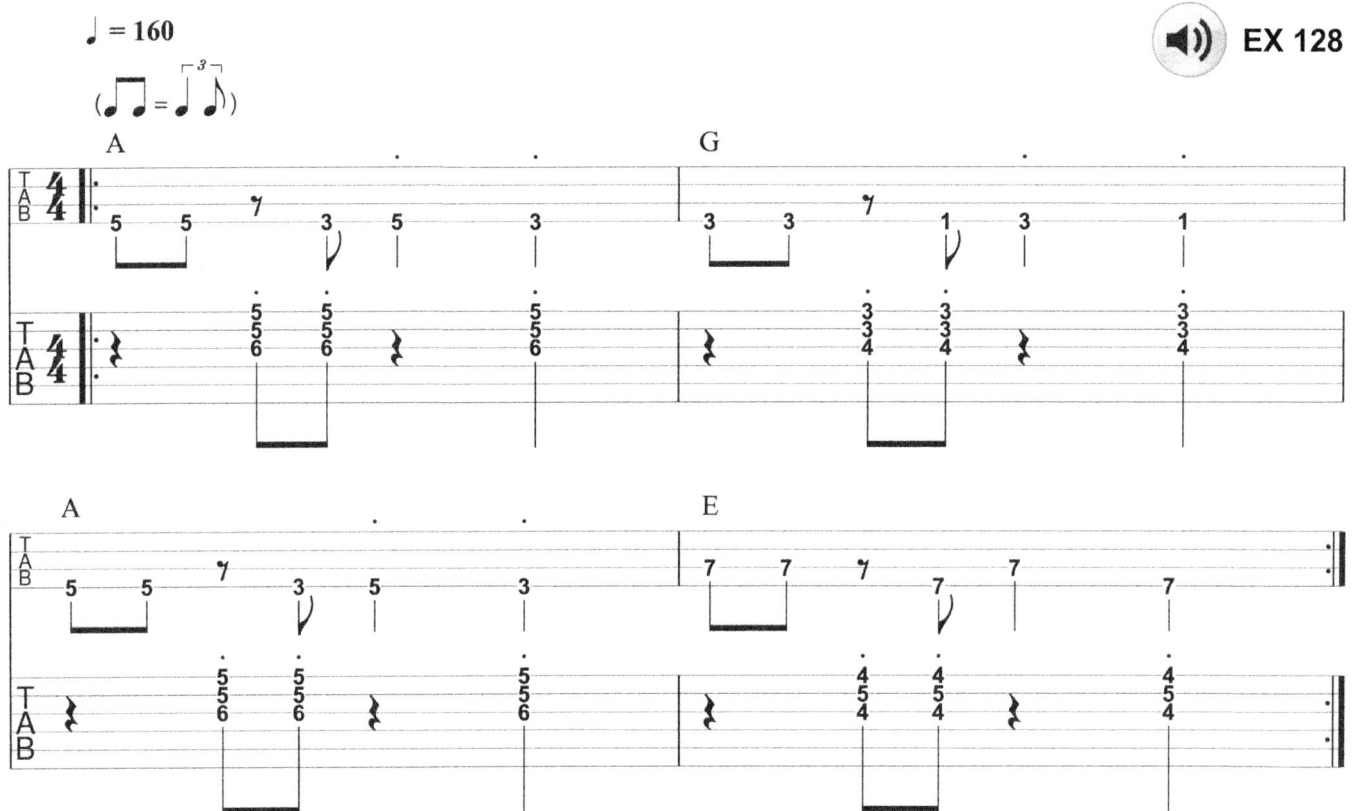

Again, by keeping the guitar part simple, it stays out of the way of the groove, which is predominantly established by the bass. If you were to play something with equal rhythmic complexity, the listener would struggle to decide which instrument is the focal point—and that's not good!

FUNK GROOVE

Let's wrap up this chapter with a genuine funk groove, which can pose a real challenge for rhythm guitarists and songwriters. The bass groove below is a popular octave figure that implies an E–G–A–B (I–♭III–IV–V) progression—another set of non-diatonic changes.

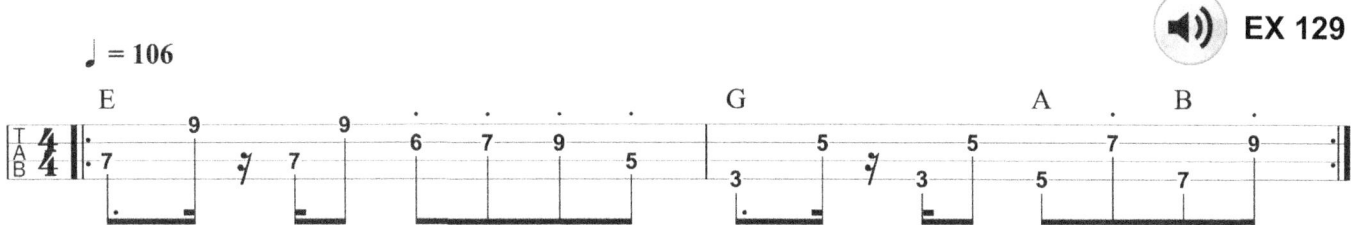

As general rule, the more complex the drum and bass groove, the simpler you should keep your guitar part. With that in mind, the figure below features a simple E–B (root–5th) dyad that is played in a syncopated rhythm throughout. Instead of following each chord change, the guitar reinforces the key center, E major, while locking in with the bass line (notice how the chord strums closely match the bass accents on strings 1–2).

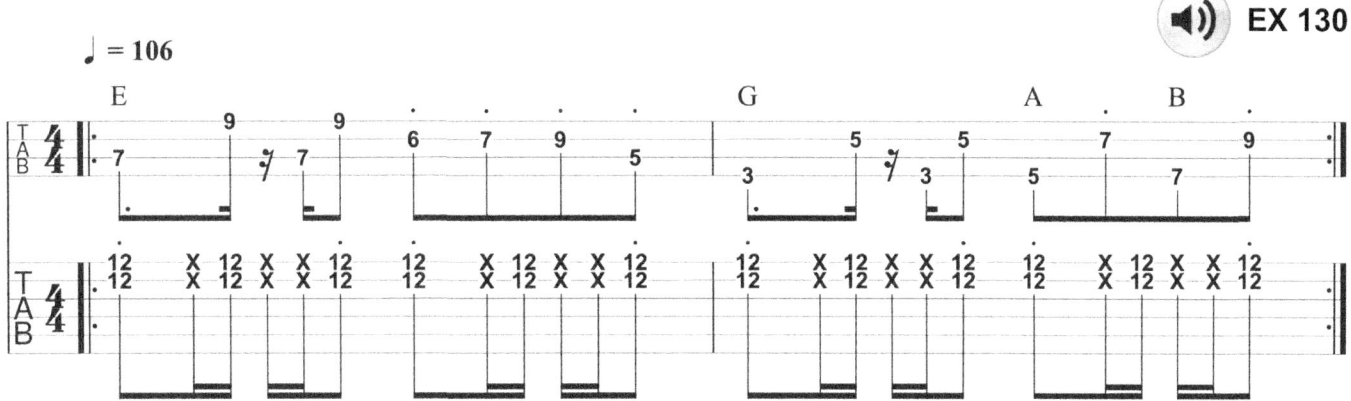

The best piece of advice for building guitar parts around a bass line is to use your ears. If things start to sound cluttered, or you're struggling to lock into the groove, then you probably need to come up with a different part. When it feels right, you'll know that you've found the right part! Again: *simple* is almost always the best solution.

CHAPTER 16: BUILDING GUITAR PARTS AROUND A DRUM GROOVE

For our last chapter, we're going to focus on how to build guitar parts around a drum groove. As mentioned in the previous chapter, sometimes great song ideas come from a groove that the drummer spontaneously creates in a jam session. If you ever find yourself in this situation, use the following tips to help you create the perfect guitar part.

TWO-BEAT FEEL

Like the bass lines in the previous chapter, the drum grooves in this chapter get progressively more complex. We'll start with perhaps the most universal drum groove of all: the two-beat feel. The *two-beat feel* features the kick drum on beats 1 and 3, and the snare on beats 2 and 4, or backbeat:

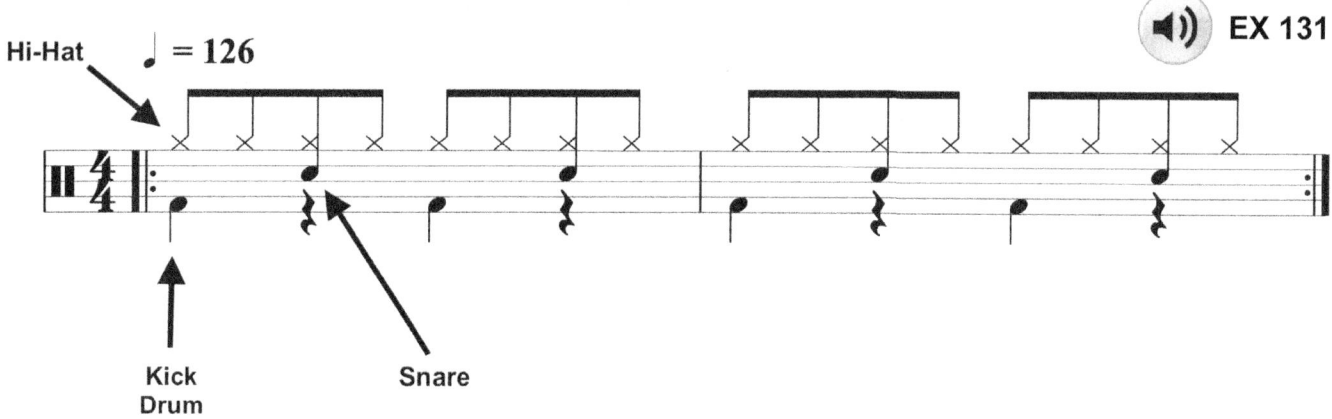

Since this is a pretty straightforward beat, we can get pretty creative with our guitar part without fear of interfering with the groove. One approach we could take is to play a relatively fast harmonic rhythm, like this:

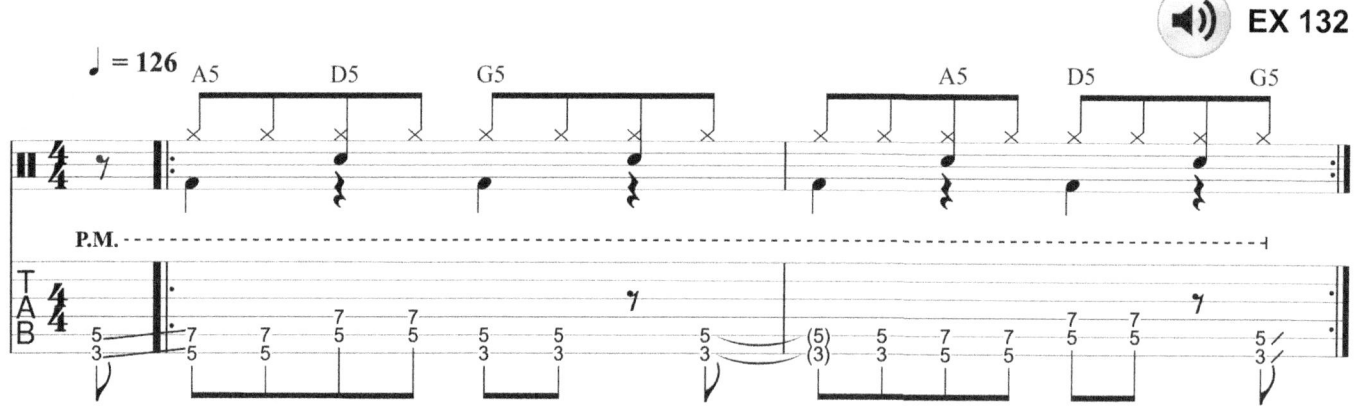

Notice that, in the example above, three chord changes are occurring per measure and a touch of syncopation (on the "and" of beat 4 in measure 1) and some well-placed rests create rhythmic interest. Without the rests and syncopation, the guitar would just be locked in with the eighth-note rhythm of the hi-hat—and that would get rather stale after a while.

SYNCOPATED GROOVE

Let's try another drum groove. The one below is similar to our previous groove, only now the kick drum is played in syncopated fashion, with several of the hits occurring on the off-beats.

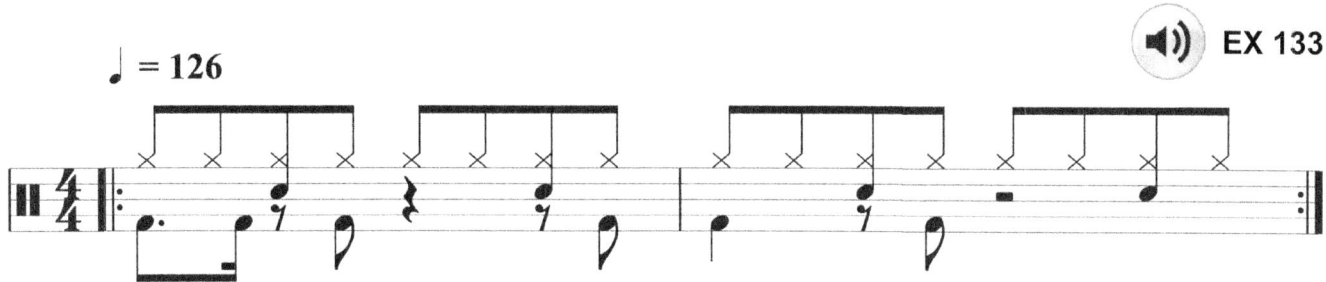
EX 133

You can try a couple of things for this type of beat: 1) you can compose a progression whose chords change on every kick-drum accent, or 2) you can strum the chords of your progression in a steady eighth-note rhythm to match the hi-hat. Let's try both methods. Here's an example of the first method:

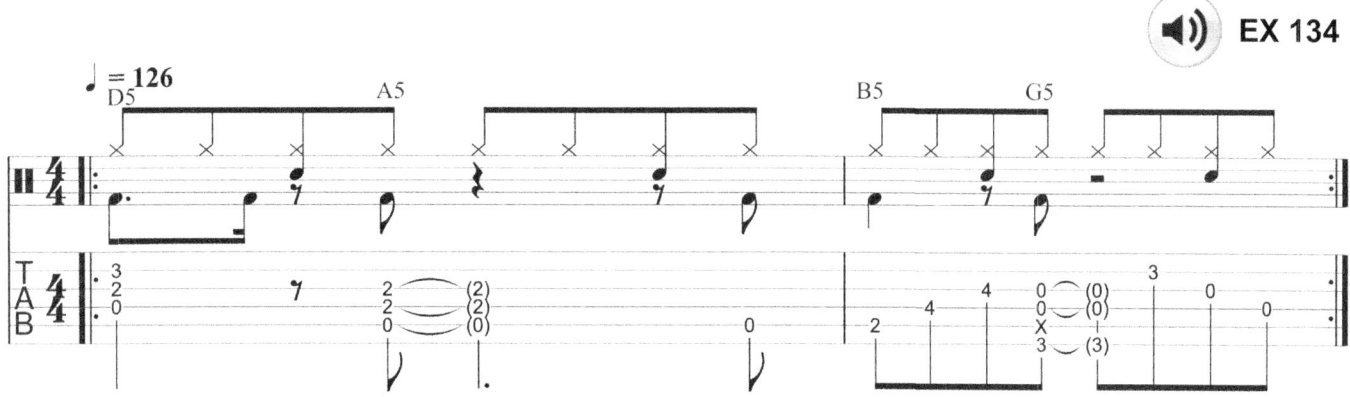
EX 134

Notice that the chord changes lock in with the kick drum in both measures, particularly on the "and" of beat 2. In situations like this, where the kick drum is providing such a strong, syncopated groove, the guitar part should enhance the beat. In other words, simpler is usually better in these scenarios.

Now let's look at another method you can use over this drum groove. Below is a simple eighth-note strumming pattern featuring open D, A, Bm, and G chords (a I–V–vi–IV progression in D major)—the same changes implied in our previous example.

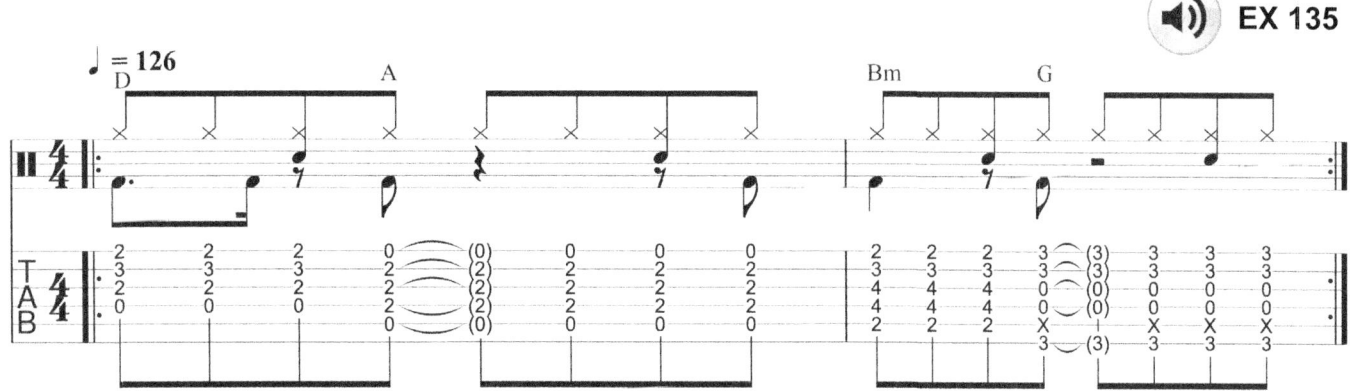
EX 135

Notice, once again, how the changes mimic the kick drum, and how the eighth-note strumming stays out of the way of the kick-and-snare groove by locking in with the hi-hat. Simple yet powerful!

HALF-TIME FEEL

One groove that enables the guitarists to really stretch out and shine is the half-time feel. The *half-time feel* is a beat that sounds like the tempo is half as fast as it really is—hence "half-time feel." This is achieved by only playing the snare on beat 3 (instead of on beats 2 and 4) and altering the kick-drum pattern in a similar fashion. Consequently, the eighth-note rhythm that the hi-hat is playing now sounds like a steady stream of 16th notes. This type of beat provides the rhythmic foundation of trap music.

Let's say your drummer comes up with the following half-time feel:

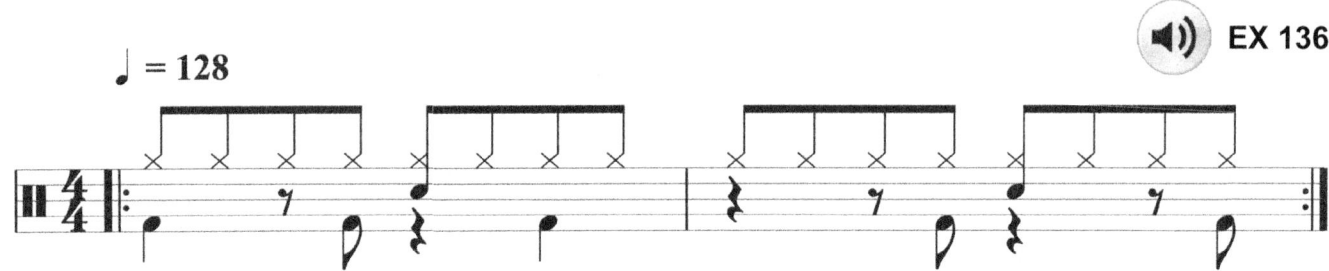

EX 136

The tempo of that beat is 128 beats per minute (BPM), but it feels like 64 BPM. Because of this slower feel and the straight-ahead nature of the beat, the guitar part can be the complete opposite. In other words, you can create a part that's more complex than simple, including adding syncopation and a faster harmonic rhythm. Below is just one option for this type of groove:

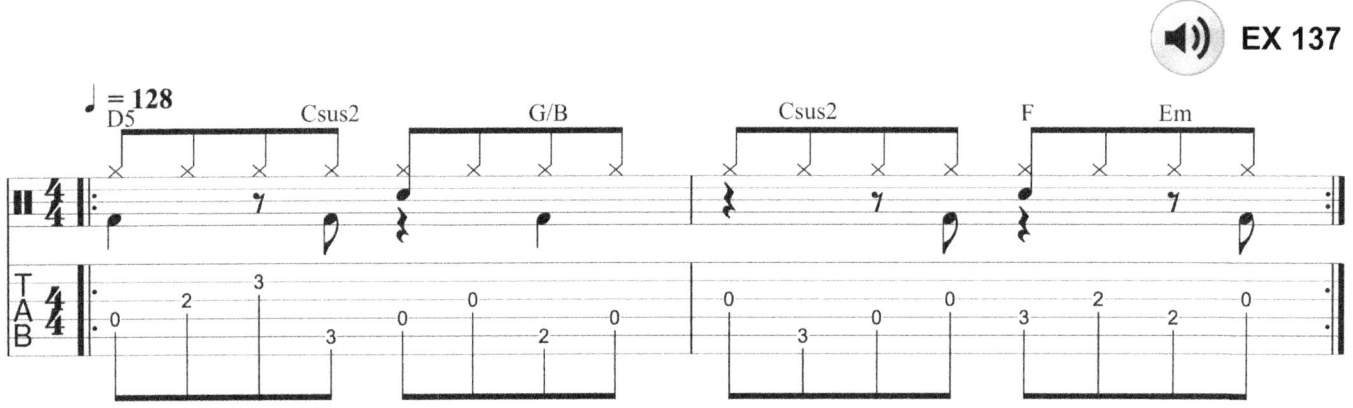

EX 137

Notice how the chords lock in with the kick drum in measure 1, changing on the "and" of beat 2 and on the downbeat of beat 4. Also note the swift pace of the harmonic rhythm, with chords changing multiple times per measure.

6/8 GROOVE

Let's wrap up this chapter with one last drum groove. Up to this point, we've been working in 4/4 time, but let's say your drummer comes up with a cool 6/8 groove, or perhaps you find a drum loop that you want to write to and it's in 6/8, like the one below:

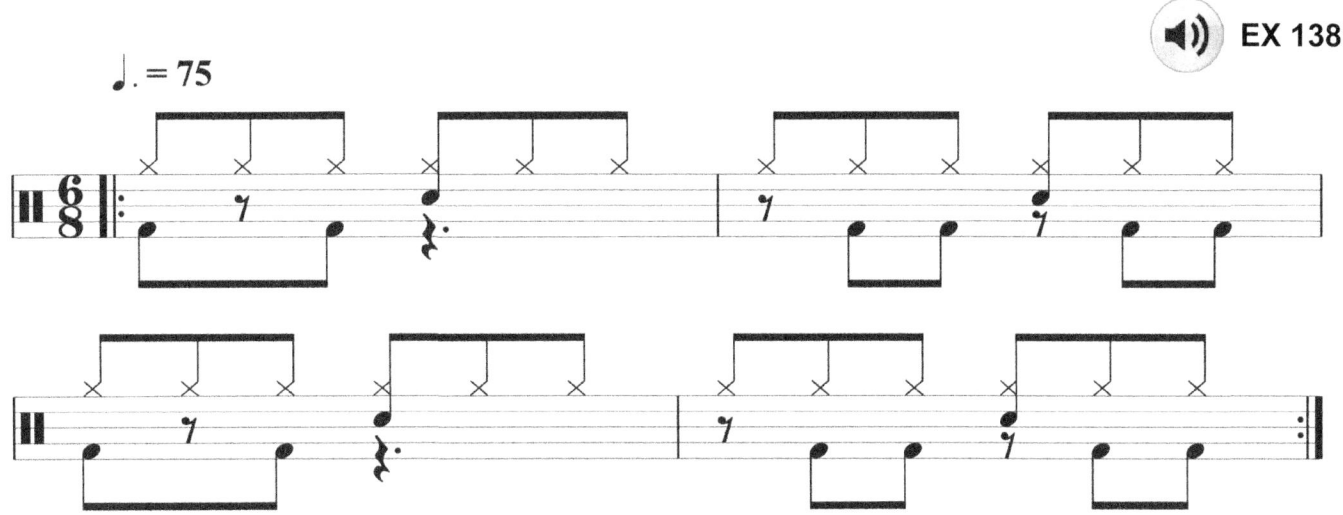

EX 138

If you look closely, you'll notice that the snare hits only once per measure (on beat 4), but the kick is rather active, especially in bars 2 and 4. For a groove like this, you could build a riff around the rhythm of those kicks. For example, you could create a rhythmic hook by accentuating those kicks with something like this:

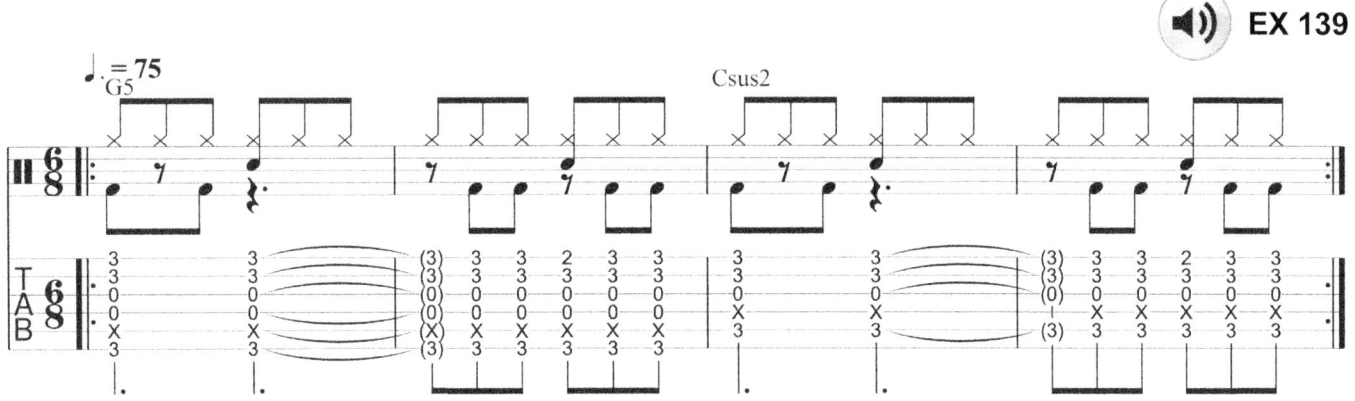

EX 139

Note that, not only are the chords played in rhythm with the kick in bars 2 and 4, but also include a simple little G–F#–G melody on the top string. Sounds good, right?

As guitar players, we tend to be a bit selfish, focusing solely on our instrument. But when it comes to songwriting, being cognizant of the other instruments, particularly drums and bass, when composing our parts is vitally important. As mentioned earlier in the book, only one or two instruments can take the spotlight at any one time, so simpler is usually better. Otherwise, they're just competing for space, and that will turn off listeners quickly. That said, don't be afraid to come up with some intricate riffs or progressions when the time calls for it. As always, let your ears be your guide!

MOVING FORWARD

I hope the tips and methods in this book have been helpful and sparked some creativity of your own. The thing about songwriting, as with anything in life, is the more you do it, the better you'll get. So, I encourage you to write as much as you can, whether you think your songs are good or bad, because you have to write a bunch of bad ones to get to the good ones. This is true for *every* songwriter, including professionals.

Although this is a guitar-focused book, I also encourage you to branch out to other instruments. I've been a guitar player for over three decades but recently began to teach myself piano so I could approach songwriting from a different perspective. And, boy, all I can say is that the results have been amazing. I'm now writing songs and composing music that I never would have a couple of years ago.

If you're interested in learning a second instrument, my publishing company, Troy Nelson Music, has put out several methods that can help, all of which are part of my *How to Play Guitar in 14 Days* series, including ones for piano, drums, ukulele, and bass guitar. All books are readily available on Amazon.

Another piece of advice I'll offer is this: learn how to record your own music! Back in 2014, after years of wanting to learn more about music production and engineering, I purchased a copy of Pro Tools, the digital audio workstation (DAW) used in most professional recording studios. Learning Pro Tools, as well as basic music recording principles, had a steep learning curve, but the time and effort I put in was well worth the benefits, because now I'm able to not only write songs, but also build full-band demos—drums, bass, keys, vocals, etc.—in my home studio. And, recently, I switched over to a different DAW, Ableton Live, and am having more fun than every building tracks, which sound infinitely better than the ones from 2014!

Moreover, producing tracks on laptops and in home studios is now the norm. In fact, a large percentage of songs you hear on the radio these days—especially pop—are produced entirely on a laptop. And even songs that were tracked in professional studios will often incorporate elements from demos that were produced in a home studio. There are two main reasons for this: 1) songs can be produced quickly, which is beneficial for all involved (artists, labels, publishers, songwriters, etc.), and 2) it's considerably *cheaper* because no professional studio is involved, and no musicians need to be hired.

So, if you aspire to write songs professionally, or even if you just love to compose music for your own pleasure, I strongly recommend learning how to use a DAW, several of which can be purchase for just a couple hundred dollars. A few worth checking out are Ableton Live, Apple's Logic, Avid's Pro Tools, Steinberg's Cubase, and PreSonus' Studio One.

Printed in Great Britain
by Amazon